WALKING BY FAITH
I AM! I CAN! & I WILL!

WALKING BY FAITH
I AM! I CAN! & I WILL!

The Story of How Joe L. Dudley, Sr.
Walks By Faith

Joe L. Dudley, Sr.

Published by Executive Press

Library of Congress Cataloging in Publication Data

ISBN 0-939-975-11-4

Barclee Cosmetics
1080 Old Greensboro Road
Kernersville, North Carolina 27284

Printed in the United States of America

FAITH

Don't let anyone turn you around,
Keep your feet on solid ground.
As long as you continue to do your best,
Whatever you do, you'll be a success.

You may get discouraged sometimes,
You might even want to cry,
But always remember,
To hold your head up high.

Sometimes life is full of disappointment,
Sometimes it is full of pain,
But as long as you keep your faith in God,
Success you'll surely gain.

There have been many mountains I thought
I couldn't climb,
But I ended up climbing most of them,
Once I made up my mind.

I have dreamed many dreams that never came true,
And when I thought all hope was gone,
God stepped in and gave me the will to make me
Want to keep dreaming on.

I have prayed many prayers that went unanswered,
Even though I was patient and waited so long.
But the Lord has answered enough of my prayers,
To make me keep praying on.

I have trusted many so-called friends,
Who in the end left me to weep alone,
But I have enough true friends,
To keep me trusting on.

I have sown many seeds that fell by the way,
Seeds that the birds fed upon,
But I have enough golden sheaves in hand
To keep me sowing on.

I have known the pain of disappointment,
And I have gone many days without sun,
But I have sipped enough nectar from the
Roses of life to make me want to live on.

No matter what your goal in life,
No matter what you do,
As long as you keep faith in God,
He will see you through.

—Stephanie Penny
Cosmetologist, Joliet, Illinois

**This book is dedicated to the memory
of S. B. Fuller:
My Mentor, My Friend,
My Inspiration!**

The biography of S. B. Fuller, "Pioneer in Black Economic Development," reads like a saga of American ingenuity. It is proof of his personal precept that financial independence can be achieved through set direction and hard work.

Born on June 4, 1905, in Monroe, Louisiana, Fuller was 22 years old when he hitchhiked to Chicago. After working first in a coal yard and then with an insurance company, he began his own business with a capital investment of $25.

Fuller Products Company was incorporated a year later. Thousands of men and women were trained in door-to-door selling and countless others were inspired to start their own businesses and go on to undreamed-of success.

Fuller's leadership greatly influenced Chicago minorities in the '40s and '50s. As his business prospered, he purchased other companies, including newspapers, a department store, and a theater. His interests also included farming and cattle ranching.

Business and public-service organizations sought him as a speaker; his achievements were the subject of news articles and books. His numerous philanthropies included charitable and scholarship funds, and he helped finance many minority enterprises.

"Convinced that anyone endowed with such determination, faith, and love of his fellowmen is worthy of the highest respect, the state of Illinois proclaims June 4, 1975, the 70th anniversary of his birth, S. B. FULLER DAY."

—Taken from the State of Illinois Proclamation
Issued by Dan Walker, Governor of the State of Illinois
The Third Day of June, 1975

ACKNOWLEDGMENTS

———

When I pray, I say "thank you, thank you," because I know that gratitude leads to plenty.

I thank God for being a God who pays all who labor in His vineyard. A God who holds all justice in His hands. A God who is never broke. A God who meets my every need.

I thank God for Dudley Products Company and for each and every product that sustains our business. I thank God for our loyal customers, employees, and many, many friends.

I thank Him for people from all over the world who have contributed to our success and made it possible for others to find true happiness in their lives.

I thank God for helping us find loyal, enthusiastic cosmetologists. I thank Him for our partnership with cosmetologists, and for letting that partnership grow into a powerful worldwide economic force.

I thank God for the best sales force in the world: The Dudley Products Professional Route Sales and Tele-Selling Managers.

I thank Him for delivering to our doorsteps talented people who are eager to carry the Dudley Mission all over the world.

I thank God for helping us build the Dudley Cosmetology School System (DCSS) and for making it possible for so many people to enhance their professional skills.

I thank Him for sending us determined students, supportive educators, and efficient administrators, all of whom are committed to making the DCSS the World Headquarters of Cosmetology.

I thank James (Jim) Harper of Harfam Management Services, Inc., both for helping me to start this book project when he worked in our Marketing Department, and for returning to assist us in the organization, editing, and book-marketing activity needed.

I thank God for my wonderful employees, cosmetologists, customers, friends, and those who have helped along the way.

Also, special thanks to Steve Williford, LaTonya Broome, John Raye, Dr. Willie Bailey, Tom Pope, and others who helped with editing.

I thank God for my wife, Eunice, who has stuck by me, given me inspiration, and been the voice of reason over the past 35 years as I have pressed toward the mark of making a difference in the world.

I also thank God for my children, Joe Jr., Ursula, and Genea, who grew up in the company and are working hard to help fulfill my dream. I love you, thank you, and appreciate each of you.

A special thank you to my brothers and sisters, all 10 of you. I could not have developed and built Dudley Products Company and the opportunity it provides to raise people without your strong assistance and support. You advised, you suggested, you sold products, and lent me money or invested money in this mission. I especially want to express my deep appreciation to my youngest sister, Elsie, for the many hours, including weekends, she spent typing and helping me to edit this book. Elsie, I could not have done it without you. Thanks.

Again, thanks, and I salute you all. You are not only my brothers and sisters; you are also my best friends.

And most of all, thanks to my mother, Clara and my late father, Gilmer.

TABLE OF CONTENTS

———

INTRODUCTION

———

Who could ever have guessed? We started mixing products in our kitchen. Now we have grown to have impact on economic and business development on an international level. Who could have guessed? Certainly not I. My life goes to show that there is no limit to how far just one good idea can take a person.

I get an incredible feeling of excitement thinking about the different roads that have been opened up to me over the years. My world has grown from being a farm boy, a worker in a chicken-processing plant, a door-to-door salesman, a creator of my own products, and now, the owner of a company that is taking the international market by storm. What could possibly come next? I say, "Absolutely anything!" Because through faith, all things are possible.

Keep the faith.

I pray that, in some small way, this book will add a new dimension to your life. Additionally, I hope it will cause you to feel that God has a purpose for your life. I want you to be excited about uncovering that purpose. There is something very special in store for you if only you will believe, in faith, that all things are possible. As you think about where you will grow from here, I challenge you to dream big.

Take it one step at a time, but set your sights high. Without vision, you cannot prosper. Remember, first the word, then the thing. Above all, take action. Go to work. You won't become a millionaire by hanging around the bank. You won't become a pilot by walking around the airport. Determine what you want in life, and then go after it! I open this book by wishing you Godspeed in achieving your dreams. Always remember: I Am! I Can! & I Will! Walk by Faith!

I strongly believe that the work we are doing at Dudley Products, Inc. is beneficial to everyone, especially to cosmetologists. It gives them renewed hope. Our work shows them that wealth and success are attainable goals. It shows them that sustaining a mission is quite possible.

Whenever I feel a moment of doubt or defeat, all I have to do to overcome any negativity is to consider just how far I've come in life. Life is exciting. We never know where the path will lead. So if you're a small-business person just starting out, be encouraged. You have a lot to learn and a great journey before you. Set your goals. Write them down. Revise them when necessary. But most important, keep the faith!

My wife and I really have fun in our business. We work long hours and always have. There's no such thing as a 9:00 a.m. to 5:00 p.m. schedule when you're serious about work and committed to it. We learned years ago that to be truly successful in accomplishing our goals, we have to be flexible. If that means working weekends, we do it. If that means working holidays, we do it.

It's not uncommon to pass by our corporate headquarters in the evenings or on weekends and see Eunice's car or mine parked out front, along with those of several of our employees. Our employees are very committed people, who go beyond the call of duty to make sure that all of our work gets done. We are all very serious about our mission, and the excitement is evident. We work because we want to.

Eunice and I don't work as hard as we do just to get a paycheck. We have learned that if we simply love and enjoy our work, the money will follow. We chose to go into business to do more than make money. We did it to render service to others. If it were just about money, we would have retired years ago. My wife and I would be in the Bahamas or somewhere else, living it up. But we want to serve as examples for our employees. We want them to share our commitment and love to help others.

"I rarely take vacations," I respond, when people ask me how much time off I take a year. Usually, people take vacations so they can do things they enjoy. I enjoy work, so coming into the office is plenty of vacation for me. My wife and I own a beautiful home in Florida, but it's rare that we have the time to stay in it.

"The termites are the only ones who stay there on most nights," Eunice and I usually remark when people inquire about our Florida home. We're very grateful but our real joy is working. So we spend most of our time at the office.

Do you enjoy your work? Are you fully invested in what you do? I'm not talking about being monetarily invested. I mean are you personally invested in your work? Does it get you excited? Are you contributing to the success of your company? Work should be an expression of your right to the pursuit of happiness. After all, why should you devote 40 hours a week for 52 weeks a year to a job that doesn't make you happy? If you can do better somewhere else, then you owe it to yourself to leave.

You'll feel a greater sense of accomplishment if you enjoy the efforts that will lead you to wealth and success. Complaining will solve none of your problems. Finding excuses won't help either. Besides that, a bad attitude will become evident in your work. You'll lose initiative. You'll feel as though everything you do is a big waste of time. Why fall into a boring pattern of merely existing while people all around you enjoy more fulfilling lives?

In 1995, Eunice and our daughter Ursula attended the International Women's Conference in Beijing, China. They met women from all over the world. They saw and talked with women from many different countries and walks of life. After they returned, Ursula told me that she could summarize with one word all that she learned from her experience in China: *Grateful!* She said it was a mind-boggling experience to meet women who never had the chance to go to school or to work, or to make decisions about their lives. She felt truly grateful to be born in the United States—a land of plenty.

Ursula said that hearing these women talk about their lives made it easier to understand why so many who come as immigrants to our country succeed in establishing profitable businesses. They are hungry for the opportunity to improve their conditions. Many of them come from countries in which it's common for six or seven people to live in a one-bedroom apartment. They have little concept of privacy. Some are forced into lifestyles of subservience and obedience. Ursula also said that several of the women admitted to being unhappy in marriages. They felt trapped, because they lacked the education and skills to provide for themselves should they leave their mates.

On the other hand, Ursula left China with a much greater sense of appreciation for the opportunities women have in the United States. She concluded that often we take these opportunities for granted. Some people just do enough to get by. They do not fully utilize their God-given talents.

Just imagine what these women thought of my wife, the chief financial officer of our company, and my daughter, our corporate counsel. But the essence of this story is that all too often the people with the most opportunity take it for granted.

Challenge yourself to take advantage of your talents. Develop the "Divinity" within you. Seek out a career and a lifestyle that motivates you. Get hungry for the opportunities right under your nose. Remember, as author Russell Conwell puts it: You may live on *Acres of Diamonds.*

I know how the pattern sets in, because it's happened to me. But I took control of the situation and resolved to make some changes. Life is far too short to waste it away grumbling and complaining. It pays to be excited about what you do, especially if you must work to maintain yourself and your family. So you might as well do something that you enjoy.

I have met some very smart people since starting in business. Some of them have had excellent business ideas. Some have had good intentions about ways to make their lives better. However, many of them never took action. They would latch on to every excuse imaginable instead of just taking advantage of their creative energy. They let negative thoughts stifle their best plans. Worse yet, they had positive talk but not action. You must walk the talk!

I challenge you not to be like these people. Find out what you enjoy, and then do it. If you need more training, then get it. It's worked for virtually every millionaire in the country, and I'm certain that it will work for you. Come with me now as I share with you the way faith and hard work led me and made possible the development and success of Dudley Products.

A Family Affair

Betty Clawson, Director
Dudley Beauty College
Chicago, Illinois

I first met Mr. Joe L. Dudley, Sr. some 27 years ago when my older brother, Johnny, invited me to a Saturday morning Sales Meeting. My brother worked his way through school selling Fuller and Dudley Products door to door. I was 28 years old and married with one daughter, Terrie. With a full-time job at Southern Bell Telephone Company and the day-to-day responsibilities of running a home, I decided to take my daughter on a week-end trip to Greensboro, North Carolina. Terrie could visit her cousins and I could attend the CIAA Basketball Tournament. This would be a change from spouse and mother duties. Of course, I told my husband I was going to the sales meeting with my brother. Little did I know that the excuse I was using to get to the game would result in the most important day of my life.

Saturday morning at Dudley's 717 East Market Street location was no ordinary experience. Even though I was reluctant to go to this meeting, I was curious as to why my brother was so enthusiastic about selling cosmetics. He expressed more excitement about going to the meeting than going to the game and seeing our old friends. I recall that as we entered the building bright and early that winter morning, we were greeted by a spunky, cheerful individual. Emphatically she instructed "Johnny, go on back! Go on back! A demonstra-

tion is going on!" I was truly impressed that the individual sending the sales people to the meeting room so aggressively was Mrs. Eunice Dudley herself.

*During the meeting, a young man by the name of James Cheek gave a remarkable speech on **Mr. Triumph and Mr. Defeat**. He won my individual attention as he delivered his inspirational message. Next, Mr. Dudley spoke to the group. He talked about being on a mission to change the world. His desire to spread Dudley and Fuller Products all across the country was so evident I became convinced that I had to be a part of this financial empowerment program. Before I left that day, I had purchased a $10.00 sales kit and was ready to travel to Charlotte, North Carolina to assume my role in this new venture.*

I did not plan to leave my job at Southern Bell Telephone Company, but I could surely expose friends and family to this wonderful opportunity. Recruiting others was no challenge because everyone I talked to bought into the mission of self-sufficiency. My crew grew so fast that Mr. Dudley asked me to open up a branch in Charlotte. He said, "You are currently making $97.50 a week. I want to give you more than they are paying you. I will pay you $100.00 per week." I took a leave of absence from the telephone company with the intention of returning after the branch was established. Needless to say, I never returned to that job.

Although the education and personal growth I received selling door to door was phenomenal, generating revenue in a start-up business created additional expenses for the household. I sold, invested in my own inventory, and also managed the operation. I was fully committed to helping to make this dream become a reality. I remember one particular day after picking Terrie up from cheerleader practice, we went out to one of the neighborhoods to sell. The objective was to collect enough money to buy a box of hamburger helper and some ground beef to make dinner that evening. Times were lean but we were believers.

Mr. Dudley saw my sincerity and introduced me to Mr. S. B. Fuller. He exposed my weaknesses to Mr. Fuller. The main one that

inhibited my personality was my fear of being hurt and embar-
rassed. For example, I would respond to embarrassing situations
with tears. Mr. Fuller told Mr. Dudley, "If you can stop Betty from
crying, she can become a great lady. You see, crying denotes defeat."
I believed him. One deficiency prohibiting my success was those
tears, so I used all the strength I could muster to overcome my im-
maturity.

As I grew personally in my life and professionally as a manager,
so did the branch as well as sales. Mr. Dudley, with his strong belief
in self-sufficiency, felt every manager should earn a percentage of
the business. This gave me a sense of ownership. "Oh, what a job to
have the freedom to make a business grow and give opportunities at
the same time." Then along came my second child, Sherri. While I
was in the hospital, my husband George opened the mail and dis-
covered how much money I was being paid. His ego was injured. He
called Mr. Dudley and told him "How dare you pay my wife more
money than I make." He wanted a wife with whom he felt he did not
have to compete. Mr. Dudley called me and told me to invest in an
Eldorado Cadillac car for George. This model was more expensive
and more luxurious than the elegant car I had purchased for myself.
Even though I complied with Mr. Dudley's request, my husband did
not perceive the car as a token of my appreciation for his support.
We eventually divorced. Mr. and Mrs. Dudley were extremely sup-
portive of my needs as well as the spiritual and moral development
of Terrie and Sherri. I was permitted to produce and direct television
and radio commercials as well as perform public relations responsi-
bilities for the company. My daughters were able to see me excel in
spite of personal disappointment and failure. God always gives us
what we need, when we need it. Dudley Products was the vehicle to
give me the sense of value that I needed.

In the midst of all the challenges associated with establishing a
factory in a different state, I called the Dudleys seeking comfort af-
ter the end of another disappointing relationship. Inventory was
scarce due to the relocation, but we had to believe that, "This too
shall pass."

Introduction

I went to an auction, solely for motivation, and boldly placed a bid on a house. The auction wanted 10% as a down payment. Since I had some money invested in Dudley Products, I asked Mr. Dudley if it was possible to get some of it back. I explained to him I knew this was not the best time as the expense of the factory move was most important to all of us. I told him I could renege on my offer if the company could not afford it at this time. He said, "Absolutely not. God directed you to that house and that house is yours." The money was there within 24 hours. That incident is so precious to me. I was so touched. I remember thinking to myself "Gee, this man values the personal happiness of his employees more than the immediate needs of the company."

There is another time in that particular era where Mr. Dudley was there for me. A teacher from the middle school where my daughter was enrolled notified me that she was not going to pass her grade. I began to feel guilty as if I had neglected some of my responsibilities. One day while I was at work, Mr. Dudley called my house and Sherri answered the telephone. She told him about her situation and he told her to repeat the phrase, "I am! I can! and I will!" over and over again. He instructed her to repeat that phrase whenever she felt inadequate about accomplishing a task. She not only passed her grade, but was given the opportunity to participate in many other activities at the school. Her personality became very outstanding.

Today, I am Director of the Dudley Beauty College in Chicago, Illinois and both my daughters work with the company. In fact, neither of them have ever worked anywhere else. I am especially grateful for the opportunity that the Dudleys have given to my daughters. The education and personal growth they obtained while working in Brazil, South America is immeasurable. Working with the Dudley International Exchange Program forced them to become bilingual in order to survive and gave them appreciation for many cultural experiences. I am totally convinced that the success that we have enjoyed as a family is a direct result of the patience, guidance, and direction of Dr. Joe L. Dudley, Sr.

"Fool Them Joe, Prove Them Wrong"

On May 9, 1937, I was born the fifth of 11 children to Gilmer and Clara Dudley. I was named after Joe Louis, the famous boxer. My aunt chose the name. She said that being named after somebody important might actually rub off on me. My parents must have liked her thinking, because they named three of my brothers after legendary people as well: Alfred Degreat, MacArthur, and George Washington, after a King, the General, and the first president.

We grew up in the small town of Aurora, North Carolina, a farm community where the wealth of a family was often measured by the success of the land they tended. Opportunity and resources were scarce, but since most people had never lived anywhere else, they didn't know any different.

Growing up on a farm, we were taught not to fear hard work. My parents were hard-working people, and they passed that characteristic on to each of us. My parents valued education, and required each of us to attend and complete college. Growing up poor taught us that going to school was a privilege. There were many times when we couldn't go at all because of all the work to be done.

My parents had no choice but to give basic necessities higher priority than going to school. Sometimes we'd get up early in the morning, hoping to get a jump start on our chores so we'd finish in time to go to school. But no matter how early we got up or how much we did, there always seemed to be something else for us to do. During the farming time of the year, the only time we got to go to school was when it rained.

They Were Right, I Was Retarded!

From the very beginning, I had a hard time adjusting to school. I couldn't stay focused on what we were being taught, so I spent most of my time telling jokes and pulling pranks and getting into trouble. I got a whipping for one thing or another practically every day. It got to the point that I just didn't care. After a while, I got used to the whippings and would sometimes do silly things on purpose just to get whipped for attention.

I liked, above all, being able to make other kids laugh. Being the class clown took away some of the embarrassment I felt about the way I talked. I had a speech impediment, and there were times when kids would poke fun at me. Joking around was my way of getting other people to laugh *with* me and not *at* me. Nobody ever gave much thought to the fact that I was feeling insecure.

Unable to understand or control my behavior, the school personnel told my parents that I was mentally retarded. Even though my parents didn't tell me that I had been labeled mentally retarded until many years later, they couldn't hide the fact that my teacher retained me in the first grade.

Falling Behind

One year, when I was around 9 or 10, my grandmother became very ill. My aunt, who lived with her, worked nights, thus leaving my grandmother home alone most evenings. My mother was concerned about grandmother being left alone, so she sent me to stay with her every evening. I enjoyed having extra freedom. There was nobody checking up on me, making sure my homework was done or asking what I'd learned in school that day. I became very slack about school. I didn't do my work and even started to skip school some days.

I was retained again that year. This time around, my parents weren't understanding. On the first day of the new school year, Mother sent a note to my teacher saying that she and Daddy didn't send me to school to play, and that they fully expected me to make my grade after being in school all year long. Both my parents and the teacher stayed on my case all year. Mother even had my sister, Martha, who was younger than I, but in the same grade, checking up on me at school. There were even times when Martha's test papers were accessible to me. I took full advantage of that, for she had very good study habits. I did what I had to do to get by. Martha's good study habits took her on to Tuskegee University in Alabama and to Fordham University in New York, where she earned a Master's degree in social work. At this writing, she holds an administrative position with the city of New York's Department of Human Resources Administration.

That Smart Boy Took My Girlfriend

Everything changed my junior year in high school, when a single event led me to clean up my act. I was dating one of the most beautiful girls in school. Her family lived in Blounts Creek, a small town near Aurora. Having her for my girlfriend made me all the more popular. We dated for almost two years. I would walk more than 12 miles some weekends to her house, just to court. I was so into our relationship that I had already talked to my mother about getting married.

It was my first real love, and I was into it head over heels. Then one day, out of the clear blue sky, my girlfriend dumped me for another boy. She came right out and said, "Joe, I don't want to date you anymore. I like somebody else." It was the last thing on earth that I expected to happen. The love of my life was rejecting me, and it really hurt. I responded, "But why? I'm a nice guy. What could you possibly see in somebody else?"

I desperately wanted to know what was so wrong with me. When she told me who her new boyfriend was, I shouted, "My goodness, he's ugly. Surely, you can see that he's ugly."

"Well, maybe so, Joe," she replied, "but at least he's smart."

"Smart?" I repeated, as the words shot angry hurt all through my body. She was saying that I wasn't smart, and that hit a sensitive spot in me. I was tired of people thinking I was a dummy. "I can learn anything I want to learn," I yelled as I walked away.

Confused by the rush of emotions I felt, I decided to go looking for "Mr. Brains" to teach him a lesson about fooling around with my girl. How dare he try to steal her from me! I was ready for a good fight, but I couldn't find him anywhere. As my anger started to wear off, I headed home. Alone in my room, I cried my eyes out as the same words ran over and over again in my head: ". . . but at least he's smart . . . but at least he's smart . . ."

For the first time in my life, I came face-to-face with reality. Deep inside, I knew that my girlfriend was right. I spent so much time focusing on all the wrong things that I never gave much thought to learning. I had taken no interest in the things we were taught in school.

Mother's Plea: "Fool Them All Joe, Prove Them Wrong"

By the next morning, the whole town knew that I had been dumped. Some people said that they weren't surprised at all. They never understood what she had seen in me from the beginning, and they certainly didn't think that we would wind up married. The next evening, as I moped around, feeling a lot of self-pity, Mother called me into the kitchen for a talk.

"Joe," she said, "Don't let this one bad thing ruin you. You *are* a smart boy." Mother said that breaking up with my girlfriend was probably for the best. After reminding me that I had been on the verge of quitting school to marry this girl, Mother again said that I really ought to put my energy into things that nobody could ever take away from me.

"Joe," Mother said, "there are people who say to me, 'Clara, you got good kids—all except that Joe. It won't surprise any of us if Joe doesn't even make it through high school.' But I've never believed that about you. I've always believed that you could do anything you set your mind to. I believe in you. You can be somebody. I want you to fool them all!"

I will never forget that conversation with my mother, because it reminds me that, at a time when nobody was on my side, she was there for me. As a result of our little talk, I vowed to myself that I was going to change. I was going to learn something. I intended to put something in my head that nobody could ever take away.

I got all of the school books that I could find around our house and promised myself that I was going to read every one of them. I sat down with a book every night. Daddy was so excited about what I was doing that he made sure I had a good oil lamp to make my reading easier. Sometimes he would even pick up a book and sit and read with me. Although my father left school after the fifth grade, he was always an avid reader.

Learning How to Learn

I enjoyed reading and learning so many new things. As I read, I tried to focus on each word and sentence until I clearly understood. I used the dictionary to look up words that I didn't know. Reading gave me a feeling of confidence that I had never had before. I was going to prove to everyone that Joe Louis Dudley was smart!

I read my books from the first grade, and kept going: Second grade! Third grade! Fourth grade! Fifth grade! Sixth grade! Seventh grade! Eighth grade! Ninth grade! Tenth grade!

It took me a while to understand some of the things I read, but I kept trying. Any time I started to feel discouraged, my mother was there for me. She'd say, "Joe, don't you give up now. Remember: Once a slow one gets it, he's got it!"

Reading evolved into a habit that I continued throughout my life. I now believe that reading people are ruling people.

As the months passed, the embarrassment and heartache I felt after losing my girlfriend faded away. Something good had come out of my being dumped. I was finally getting my priorities in order and actually thinking about my future. It makes me smile when I think back to when my mother said, "Fool them, Joe," but that's exactly what I've done.

I've come from being a mentally retarded prankster with a speech impediment to who I am today: Joe Louis Dudley, millionaire by the age of 40 and President/CEO of one of the largest minority-owned manufacturers and distributors of professional hair and personal-care products in the United States.

So I say, "In our time, and in our space, and with the grace of God, you and I can make a difference." I have lived by this creed.

Retarded, But Not Counted Out

Jarvis Parson
Production Assistant
Manufacturing Department
Dudley Products, Inc.

I have worked for Dudley Products, Inc., for more than 10 years. In fact, my whole family relocated from Indiana to North Carolina to work for the company. When we first moved here, I managed to hold down several odd jobs with different companies. Sometimes, when I was feeling depressed, I didn't work at all. I was considered mentally retarded, a label I received when I was young. I was really angry with myself for not being smart. People would tease me, saying that I didn't know the difference between a nickel and a dime, or that I couldn't tell left from right. All I wanted was to be like everybody else. I wanted to go to college and get a good job, as everybody else in my family had done. I had no idea, until I met Mr. Dudley, that the only thing standing in my way was my attitude.

One day Mr. Dudley asked my mother how I was doing. It was during one of my periods of depression and unemployment, so my mother responded that I was not doing very well.

"Seems like he's content getting a government check every month," she said.

She told Mr. Dudley that I had no motivation to do something with myself.

Mr. Dudley told my mother to go to the Social Security office and have my disability payments stopped. He also asked her to bring

7

me to his office. Mr. Dudley told me that he too had been labeled mentally retarded when he was young. He said that if he could overcome it, then so could I. I admired Mr. Dudley for telling me that. He believed in me and, to prove it, he gave me a job cleaning one of his beauty salons. I tried my best to do a good job. I wanted Mr. Dudley to be proud of me.

Soon, I was given responsibility for cleaning two stores. Then, Mr. Jackson, a co-worker, recommended me for a job in the plant. Mr. Dudley gave me a chance at it. Since that time, I've been working in the manufacturing department.

These days I feel like a new man. I have goals for my life and things I want to do. Every morning, I'm awake by 5:00 a.m., getting ready for my day. I get dressed and cook my own breakfast. By 6:00 a.m., I'm on my way to work. With Mr. Dudley's help, I've learned to make a budget for myself, and I also keep money in a savings account. I've bought myself several business suits. I like them, because rich men wear suits. Since I plan to be rich one day, I wear them too.

Nobody calls me mentally retarded anymore. Now they just say, "Good morning, Jarvis" or "Good afternoon, Jarvis." I want everybody who has ever been labeled mentally retarded to know that you can be anything you want if your attitude is right and you accept no limitations. Mr. Dudley and I are living proof!

2

Walk by Faith

Do you want to make a difference in this world? Do you want to change the lives of other people around you? If so, then we have something in common. For as long as I can remember, I've wanted to have a positive impact on the world. I want to do more than just live an average life. I have a genuine, heart-felt desire to empower people, to raise them to a higher level of existence. The hardest thing about fulfilling this desire is knowing where to start. Perhaps you've encountered the same challenge. I will share with you several key principles, which I believe are essential to bringing about positive change and the best possible good for others. I will do this by sharing parts of my life story. I always encourage people to tell their stories. I encourage you to tell your story. It will surely help someone else, and it will help you.

First the Thought, Then the Thing

First there was the Creator, the Creative Force, or whatever you call it. First the Force spoke the Word, and then the world, the Earth, and everything else in it came into being.

A layman's version of this occurrence is, *First the thought, then the thing.* You can observe this version in just about every self-help book you can find. Certainly it resounds throughout the Bible. Remember, *"First the word, then the thing."*

Faith Makes Bad Good and Good Better

All you need to make the words manifest themselves on the material plane is Faith. Faith makes bad good and good better! You will understand this powerful concept as you read this book. By the time you finish this book, you will **know how** faith makes bad good and good better.

The Right Spirit

Webster defines spirit as: The essential nature of a person. The part of the human being associated with the mind and feelings as distinguished from the physical body.

The right spirit will attract to you everything that you need. Every creation originates in the spirit. The most important thing in business is its spirit. The most important thing in any organization, business or otherwise, is its spirit. Everything starts with spirit.

First the thought, and then the thing is the correct order for creating anything, whether it be a business, a book, or anything else. This approach is the hallmark of the wise. Wisdom is the ability to create, and successful people have wisdom.

Now let me try to illustrate this principle to you, because it is so fundamental to achieving success. A watermelon seed attracts to itself everything that it needs to become a watermelon. If the ground is cultivated properly and the weather cooperates (if sun and water come as required), the seed will attract to itself everything that it needs to become a watermelon. Surely, if this little watermelon seed can do this, then you and I can do no less.

All you have to do is to remove everything negative from your mind. Remove hatred, jealousy, envy, and all negative emotions from your mind, and you will see how God will send you the right thoughts, plans, and actions. He will not bless you if you are negative, fearful, or mean. He *will* bless you if you show love and walk by Faith.

By now you must know that you have the spirit of divinity. You must know that if God be for you, no one can be against you. You must know, as David in the Bible said, "I have been young and I have been old, but I have never seen the righteous forsaken or their seed beg bread."

I believe that what the righteous touches prospers. If you are not prospering, check out your attitude. If it's negative, watch out; you're going downhill. If it is positive, things will always turn out for the better. This I know and believe. My life is proof. Throughout this book you will see how and why things work this way. It is God's law.

Think First, Then Do

Notice that I didn't say, "first the thing, then the thought." This is inverted thinking. It rises from and leads to limited thinking. I said *first the thought, then the thing.* This type of thinking springs from and leads to the power of the infinite mind—the unlimited mind of creation. To say "first the thing, then the thought" is like saying "first the airplane, and then the thought or idea of an airplane." I have discovered that often I failed because I used the wrong thinking.

Positive Talk; Positive Actions

I have learned that you must develop a realistic plan of action. You have to know exactly what you want to accomplish and then seek out the best way to make it happen. It's best to write out your plan so that you can continuously refer back to it. By writing this down, you will also be able to chart your progress and make changes when necessary. I caution you to be sure your plan is realistic. Don't disappoint yourself by desiring too much too soon.

There is a young man named Quintin Nettles who works with our company. His parents were the first salespeople Eunice and I recruited into our company. Quintin was 12 years old when his parents came to work with us. When he got older, we hired him to sell as well. He spent a lot of time working with Mr. Fuller in Chicago. Eventually, he grew to become a good salesman. Quintin needed foot surgery several years ago and was concerned about how he would maintain his sales while he recuperated. But he didn't focus on the negative side. He knew it would be a challenge, but he focused on what he hoped to accomplish. Specifically, he didn't want to lose any sales.

Quintin got the idea to buy a pair of walkie-talkies. Accompanied by his wife, Danielle, he made his sales calls every day. Danielle would go inside the salons, and Quintin would communicate with his customers from his car, using the walkie-talkies. For 10 weeks, Quintin and his wife called on clients this way. He didn't lose a single sale. He kept up his goal. He focused on the positive side and got positive results. You are most creative when you are positive.

While nothing is impossible, most things worth planning require time to be properly implemented. You must be realistic. You must also be genuine. Check your motives to be sure that you are not setting out to do great things solely for the recognition that may come to you. If you are after money, fortune, or fame, then you are not out to help others; you're out to help yourself. Don't fool yourself and, for the love of people, don't go around trying to fool others. Eventually, your genuine motivation will show through. If it is positive, you prosper. If it is negative, you will most often not prosper.

Gratitude Leads to Plenty

Ask yourself: "What do I want? Why do I want it?" Write it down. Next, learn to be grateful and not full of pride. If you want to make a difference, if you want to be successful, get in the habit of saying "Thank You." Certainly say thank you to God every day. I prefer *gratitude* to pride. Gratitude is realizing that you didn't make it this far in the world all by yourself. Others have helped you along the way. Pride, on the other hand, is believing that nobody has contributed anything to your learning and growth; that you did it all on your own.

Pride Goeth Before a Fall

False pride is living a lie. It's failing to acknowledge that somebody long before you fought, cried, and prayed for every right you have today. If you are truly grateful, then you don't mind giving thanks for everything you have accomplished and for all the things you have acquired. By showing just a little gratitude, you set yourself up for greater blessings. By the way, a great way to show gratitude is by helping others.

Always Find Your Advantage

Yesterday is gone, tomorrow has not come, we must start now!

You must also be committed and ready to seize every opportunity. Our philosophy at Dudley Products is that "In our time, in our space, and with the grace of God, you and I can make a difference." We understand that regardless of where we are, the time is always right for each of us to think, say, and do something that will make a difference in the world. Each day presents endless opportunities to bring about positive change, and we are committed to taking advantage of each one. Things are accomplished in the "now"—not yesterday or tomorrow, but in the "now."

If you want to make a difference in the world, start right now. Don't wait for tomorrow. Focus on today. As the adage goes: "Today is the first day of the rest of your life."

Each day is your opportunity for a new beginning. What will you do with this day? Will you use it to your advantage?

Make an attitude adjustment and a commitment to think positively.

I'm going to share something with you that may come as a surprise. It has to do with the difference in attitude between people who are rich and those who are poor. Having lived at both ends of the spectrum, I can personally attest to this amazing discovery.

13

Rich People Control Their Feelings

The thoughts of a poor person are centered primarily on how he feels. His feelings serve as his primary source of motivation. He thinks and acts according to how he feels at any given moment. For example, he may think "I really don't feel like working today," and his actions follow suit. He doesn't go to work. It's that simple. Or he may think that a situation he is up against is hopeless. He might say "I don't think I'll ever get out of debt." As a result, he never does. Relying on the way they think and feel is what keeps poor people poor.

Rich People Control Their Reasoning

The middle-class person, on the other hand, relies largely upon his own understanding and reasoning. His thinking goes something like this: "I must work to support my family. Therefore, I'll work 40 hours a week, buy a home that costs 2.5 times my income, and await my retirement at age 65."

His actions follow the law of observation. He concentrates on what he observes going on around him, and those observations become his primary source of motivation. Whatever the current trends indicate, the middle-class mind rushes to get on board. The middle-class person always adheres to what seems logical and what makes the most sense to him. That's why the average middle-class person generally never rises above a comfortable existence.

Rich People Operate on Faith

Rich people take chances and defy many of the laws of reason. Their motivation stems not so much from their feelings or reasonings as it does from an internal desire that is sometimes impossible to explain or justify. Their actions often seem to contradict both data and human dictates. They tend to believe that God created them to enjoy life abundantly. They have a faith, a hope, and determination embedded deep in their hearts that motivates them into action.

It may be argued that the great education system in America teaches us to live according to the middle-class way of thinking. We are encouraged to be only as good as our classmates and to subscribe to an average/normal line of reasoning. It is expected that our actions, at any particular age, can be analyzed and categorized in such a way that they follow the norm.

Think about it: the terrible two's, the rebellious teenager, the wild-at-heart young adult, the determined college student, the mid-life crisis, the seven-year itch. The list of categories goes on and on, but the bottom line is that we are all expected to be fairly predictable in nature.

Get Off the Nail

To achieve wealth, success, and personal fulfillment, we have to break out of these molds—get off the nail, so to speak. We must refuse to live according to a prescribed set of man-made characterizations. We must live, breathe, and work according to the faith that is within us. After all, to lack faith is to live in fear. Have you ever known a person to obtain wealth and success by being fearful? It doesn't happen. Faith is crucial to lasting joy. Remember, faith makes bad good and good better.

Once a man had a dog who accidentally sat on a nail and did not get off. A friend of the man visited the man during this time. Upon seeing the dog and hearing it moaning and groaning, he asked the dog's owner, "What's wrong with that dog?"

"He's sitting on a nail," replied the owner.

"Well, why won't he get off the nail?"

"He doesn't hurt bad enough yet," replied the owner, matter-of-factly. "He hurts enough to moan and groan, but not enough to get off the nail."

The dog in this story is typical of a lot of us. We complain about our situations but do nothing, because it doesn't hurt enough yet.

Once we make up our minds to do better, and have faith that we can, we can move ahead. If you want to achieve lofty goals, just get off the nail and go for it.

"Faith Without Works Is Dead"

To renew your faith, think about the things you want out of life. Write them down. Pray to God, believing that, if it be His will, you will have every good thing you pray for. Ask God to guide you toward establishing your goals. Learn to look up for your guidance—not down. Then go to work, believing, in faith, that you'll get the desires of your heart. As you know, the Bible says, "Faith without works is dead." That means that you can't just talk a good talk and everything will fall into your lap. You have to get off your rear end and do your part. You've got to walk your talk, or as I once heard a woman say, "you've got to get off your bottom to get to the top."

Belief Is the Key to Motivation

I promise that when you change your attitude and outlook, the people around you will notice a change in you. They will become motivated and inspired by you to make a difference themselves. A hot stove doesn't have to ask anybody to get warm. It's worked for me, and I'm convinced that it will work for you, too. To be motivated to do anything, you must firmly believe in what you want to accomplish. Belief is the key to motivation. Do you believe? Really believe?

Focus Upon What You Want

Professional athletes, Olympic medalists, and even some everyday sports enthusiasts have one thing in common. They focus on the good things they want to accomplish.

Can you imagine the agony a 300-pound professional football player feels as he huffs and puffs to carry his weight up and down a football field when it's 90 degrees or higher outside? Even when he doesn't look forward to practicing, he does it anyway. He does sit-ups, push-ups, wind sprints, laps, weight lifting, and iron-pumping. He devotes hours to watching tape after tape of playbacks, highlights, and mistakes. This is the less-glamorous side of the job. Away from the adoring crowds of fans in the arena, athletes spend endless hours sharpening their skills. Like a magnifying glass, you can burn a hole in any obstacle if you just focus on it long enough and hard enough. Focus is the key.

I am honored to be friends with Dave Thomas, founder of Wendy's International. Dave's successful development of Wendy's restaurants is a study in the benefits of focusing on your goals. In his book, ***Dave's Way,*** he says that in 1940, at the age of 8, he dreamed that one day he would own the best restaurant in the world. All customers would love the food, and all employees would do everything they were supposed to do. He says that most important, people would be glad to see him. This was, and still is, his focus. Today, there are more than 4,000 Wendy's restaurants generating more than $3 billion dollars in revenue annually. Wendy's service is much praised, and Dave is a welcome visitor, via his colorful television commercials, in millions of homes daily.

As an adopted child who never met his birth parents, Dave became a global success through focus, hard work, strong family values, and good business ethics. The key is a focus that began as a dream in the mind of an 8-year-old child.

Feelings Affect Attitude and Attitude Affects Results

However, every high achiever knows that studying and practicing are necessary parts of the job. It comes with the territory. They learn discipline over their bodies and feelings. Feelings affect attitude, and attitude affects results. So regardless of how they feel, they go through the motions until it becomes a habit. I have never known hard work to kill anyone. But inactivity breeds boredom. Maintain an "I Am, I Can, & I Will" attitude. Also, remember that success is an "I did," not an "I'm gonna do" concept.

A lack of specific goals can ruin a person's chances for success. When I was a young man, I clearly had no plan for my future. My only purpose was to be cool and popular. Had I never outgrown that stage, do you think I'd be a millionaire today? Absolutely not.

My brother Alfred is one of Dudley Products' best salesmen. He finished at the top of his class at North Carolina A&T State University, with an engineering degree. For more than 20 years, he worked as a design engineer for the government, creating complicated technical-instrument packages for ships. Hearing about such an accomplishment ought to make you wonder how he could have imagined such a career when his beginnings were grounded in poverty and farm work. Alfred knew what happiness meant to him, and apparently it isn't farm work. He focused on the good things he wanted out of life and went to work to find them.

Weldon Humphrey has also worked for our company for a number of years. Weldon passed up a job as the first African-American manager at Sears, Roebuck and Company to accept our commitment to help people. Why? Because he was looking for more than just an opportunity to make money and settle into an everyday job. Weldon desired to help change the world. He wanted to have an impact on the lives of people less fortunate than he. Weldon focused on the good things he wanted out of life and took advantage of the opportunities he had to obtain them.

You may wonder how our company has managed to recruit such a diverse group of talented individuals. Some of our employees turned their lives around completely after joining our company. Others were already prominent in their careers before giving it all up to join us. What's so special about the work we do? The answer is simple: We all want to make a difference in the world. We want to be in direct contact with the people most in need of our assistance. And most important, we all recognize challenges as opportunities waiting to happen. People want to be part of a real and meaningful mission. People really want to do good. Your job as a leader is to create the opportunity for them "to do good."

Create Urgency

Often, the reason we fail to achieve our dreams is that we wait until the last minute to take action. We forget to create a sense of urgency on our own. It does no good to wait for a situation to reach the point of crisis before contemplating ways to handle it. It produces a lot of stress, and believe me, I know. But by creating the urgency, we can prevent any situation from getting the best of us.

I strive to motivate my salespeople to adopt this principle in their personal and professional lives. I asked them to consider what would happen should they wait until the middle or end of the week to start working toward their weekly sales goals. All agree that the longer they wait to get started, the less likely they are to hit the mark. So I urge them to get started early. By creating the urgency at the beginning of the week, they create a win–win situation. If they get their goals by midweek, all the better for them. If there are unexpected setbacks during the week, then there's time to recover.

I remind them of the situation facing Mr. Fuller when he needed to raise $125,000 in 10 days. He created his own urgency as soon as he realized the time frame he was up against. He got busy developing a strategy. He called on several banks and other lenders. Then he went to a variety of individuals who could help him. By the end of the week, most of the hard work had already been done. There wasn't much farther to go. Mr. Fuller's goal was in sight. And because he was so close to that goal, you can just imagine the spark of motivation that came over him. I'll bet that his mind raced through a million other options he could try in order to achieve his goal.

What do you think would have happened had Mr. Fuller waited until midweek before getting started? The answer is simple: There probably wouldn't be a Fuller Products Company or, for that matter, a Dudley Products Company.

If you aspire to be wealthy, successful, and personally fulfilled, then you have to learn to deal with challenges as they arise. You have to create your own sense of urgency and not procrastinate in taking action. You must also be open-minded to the creative ideas that come to you—ideas such as making your own products. Be willing to act on faith. Test new waters; explore every option. Go to work! It will be your ticket to greater opportunity.

My Walk With Faith

Alfred Dudley
Director of Dudley Beauty College
Washington, DC

It was the 19th of March, 1935, when I was born in Aurora, North Carolina. I have 10 brothers and sisters, and when we were growing up, we had to work hard on our family farm. I began working in the cotton fields and tobacco fields at the age of about 9. And it was hard work. My mother often said that if you wanted to get out of this condition, this hard work, working in dirty clothes, and hot sun; if you wanted one day to work in an air-conditioned room and dress in suit and tie, you had to get an education.

"I might not be able to send you to school," she said, "but if you want to get out, you'd better get an education."

Well, my mother had an eighth-grade education, and that was enough—just enough—for her to know that education was what would be required for her children to get out of their current condition and be successful in life. She talked about it so often that it stuck in my mind. I mean, she drilled it into my mind.

When I was 11 years old, our home burned down. I can remember it just as if it were yesterday, and it has now been more than 50 years. When I went to bed that night, the only thing I could think about was that my schooling was over because we were homeless. No one had a house large enough to take us all in. I was at my aunt's house, and others were with another cousin. We were scattered all over the area.

21

So that night when I went to bed, I thought my schooling was over. My whole dream—my life's dream—had vanished in that fire. I couldn't sleep that night. The next morning, my father went around to all the different places we were staying and rounded us up. He called my two older brothers together and asked, "Do you all want to build a house and stop school or do you want to continue to go to school and live in this shack?" Thank God my brothers answered, "Let's go to school and live in this shack."

So we went on to school. There were many times that school would be in session for 30 days or more—a whole month—before we could start because of having to work on the farm and harvest the crops. During that time, before we could go to school, I would go to my next door neighbor, get the assignment, do homework, and send it in the next day. I had to teach myself, because I was determined that I had to get an education. To get a college degree, I knew I must first get a high-school diploma. That was weighing heavily on my mind. I worked very hard to finish high school. I worked and studied so hard, and taught myself so well, that I was valedictorian of my class. I did this in spite of the fact that my school had no library. In fact, we did not own a television or radio to keep up with current events. We frequently would go to the neighbor's house to hear Joe Louis' fights. We got our first radio when I was in high school.

I decided early on not to let anything stop me. After I finished high school, I went away to college to become an electrical engineer. And I studied. When I got to college, I felt that I was lost. All of my fellow students had been prepared to study electrical engineering, and I hardly knew what it was. No one had told me what it was, and I didn't have a library to do any research. The only thing I was told was that electrical engineering required a lot of math, and I knew I loved mathematics. Someone said that you could make a lot of money, and I knew that I wanted to make a lot of money. They also said I could wear a suit and tie, and that also got me excited.

Before I entered college, I discovered that I had to take an entrance test. I did not make a passing score on the math and English part, so I had to take remedial classes. Now, it wasn't that I didn't know the material. The problem was that I had never taken a stan-dardized test, and I had never really found a problem that I couldn't solve. When I'd reach one of the problems, I'd work on that problem until I solved it instead of leaving it and going on to another one. I could have passed the test. But all of that turned out to be an advan-tage. It appeared to be a disadvantage, but it was an advantage. Be-cause I didn't have to study for remedial math and English classes, I could spend more time studying mechanical drawing.

Mechanical drawing was also something I was not familiar with. I had never even seen the instruments. My fellow students had been prepared in high school for engineering. They had taken me-chanical drawing, and they didn't have to study as hard as I did. But having to work hard on the farm and having a strong work ethic made it no problem for me to study 17 hours a day. I had to study, because I didn't know the material; I had not been prepared for en-gineering. I remember once drawing several plates that were part of a required configuration. It took me eight hours to draw them in ink and eight seconds to mess them up. We had to draw them in pencil, then go over them in ink. I had a lot of trouble filling the ink pens. You filled them through little slits. If you put too much ink in, you got a big blob on your paper. That meant eight more hours of work, be-cause I had to sit down and do the drawings all over again. Talk about frustration! But I was determined that I was not going to let anything stop me. So I got my pencil and went back again.

While my fellow students were having parties on the weekends, I was into my books. It was easy, because I was used to working on the farm, and we worked from can't to can't: from when you can't see in the morning until you can't see at night. Hard work was something I was used to, and studying was easy compared to the hard work in the cotton fields, tobacco fields, and potato fields in North Carolina. So I worked hard, and I successfully completed the first year.

In fact, I made pretty good grades: some A's and some B's. I did pretty well, considering that I was taking a very heavy academic load. I took a heavy load because I had to take remedial English and math, and I needed to catch up. I wanted to graduate, so I could go back and help my younger brothers and sisters. My younger brother, Cornelius, now works across the street from me. I had to get out of college so I could help him. He too wanted to become an engineer. It was expected in our family that when each of us completed college, we would reach back and help the others until we all completed college.

I went back home during the summer to help my father farm. Keep in mind that my father had 11 kids, and all 11 kids were in school, ranging from elementary school to the school of veterinary medicine at Tuskegee Institute in Alabama. All of us were in school at one time, and my father had little money to help us. We all had to work our way through school. So after my first year, I went back home. I said I was going to help my father on the farm while my older brothers went away and got jobs to make money for school.

About three weeks before time for me to go back to college, my father said, "Son, I have no money."

I knew he was telling the truth, because those of you who have ever been on a farm know that if you don't have irrigation, and it doesn't rain, all your hard work is for nothing. You don't get anything. He indeed had no money. Well, I was 20 years old at the time, and I just cried like a baby. A big man crying. This was the second time that I thought the college education I had wanted so much all these years had just vanished in front of my eyes. I remember walking up and down the road, praying and asking "Now what can I do?" I thought about going into the Army, but I didn't want to go as an enlisted man. If I was going into the Army I wanted to go in as an officer. I just kind of got that out of my mind. I said, "I'm going back to school, and I'm going to have to find a way."

So I went out to get a job. Because I had worked only for my father all my life and never worked for anyone else, it was difficult for me to find a job. I had no track record.

The man I approached said "I can't hire you. I've got to hire the men I hired last year." It was seasonal work I was pursuing. Trucks would come with tobacco, and you would unload them during that particular season.

About that time, a truck drove up. If it had arrived a minute earlier, it would have been too early; if it had arrived a minute later, it would have been too late.

The fellow said, "Well, wait a minute, I'll hire you to help unload this one truck, but I won't hire you as an employee."

I said "Thank you," and I went to work on that truck. I worked harder than any man living, dead, or even unborn. He said, "I want you to stay on." He gave me a job.

Now I didn't work that way because I was trying to get the job. I didn't think I was going to get it. I worked that way all the time. See, it was a habit that I had formed. When you work for yourself, you form good habits. Most people on jobs today work only enough so that the boss won't fire them, and they get paid just enough so that they won't quit. That's about how most people go through life. But growing up on farm land was different. We knew we had to get certain things done; we had to get the crops in the ground before a certain date, had to cultivate them, and had to do certain things that had to be done, and that's how we worked.

Since I had a good work ethic, I had no problem. In three weeks I had saved $150. My entire four years of college cost only $400, so you can imagine what $150 was like more than 40 years ago. Later when I told the boss I was stopping and going back to school, he had a fit. He thought surely I was going to be there giving him that good labor for the full season. He was also happy with me though, because I probably worked as much as two men for him. During the time I worked there, I didn't spend one dime of my pay. Those days you could collect soda bottles and sell them. Soda cost you five cents. For lunch, I would take part of my bottle money and buy me a soda, and I brought my egg sandwich from home. I did not buy anything else. I saved every dime, and in three weeks I was back on my way to finishing my college education—and accomplishing my dream.

So I went back to school, not knowing where the rest of my money was coming from. I say to you today, that man's extremity is

God's opportunity. When you go as far as you can go, a power greater than man will come to help you out. And it has happened to me many times. After the $150 was gone, one of my brothers in veterinary medical school had saved money while he was in college and sent me some. Somebody else sent me a little money. I was able to complete my second year.

That summer, I had a job driving a cab. I drove a cab for a solid month without going to bed, because I was determined I was going back to school. I went back to college, and the third year wasn't as hard, because I had formed study habits.

All of my fellow students in engineering were beginning to exhaust the knowledge they had acquired in high school. Now it was necessary for them to study, and they didn't have a good work ethic. They didn't have the study habits that I had. So where were they? Where once they were making top grades, now I took over. I became the head of the class. We started with 75; we eventually graduated 15. Engineering is one of the toughest majors you can take. Many people will start, but only a few will graduate with their class.

I especially remember taking mechanical engineering. In mechanical engineering, you study forces and structures. When you're building a bridge, you have to sit down and plot all the different structure beams and so forth, and you have to calculate all components. I remember the first test I took in mechanical engineering, and I made about 45. Everyone had said that if you got through this particular course, you would be able to make it in engineering. So when I took the test and scored 45, I felt, for the third time, that my dream was over. Boy was I sick.

Well I wasn't sick for long. When I realized that was the second highest mark, I was all right. Here's what happened: The professor was from the Massachusetts Institute of Technology, and when you first started, he would give you the hardest exam he could come up with. He wanted to test us to see where we stood. One fellow made about 90. He was almost a genius, and the professor had to stop to figure out how he got those answers right. So you know I was excited to second him.

Walk by Faith

*I was on my way again! I went on with confidence, and I gradu-
ated. I graduated at the top of the 15 engineering students in my
class who went on to graduate.*

*After graduation, I got a job with the federal government. I fin-
ished college in June of 1958. I got out of class Friday evening,
boarded the bus, and went directly to Washington, D.C., from the
campus of A & T State University (known at the time as A & T College). I started work on Monday. Beforehand, I had set myself up
with two jobs. I had interviewed for and been accepted in the
Philadelphia Navy Shipyard, and for the job in Washington, D.C.,
with the General Services Administration. I decided to set up two
jobs so that in case one fell through, I could go through with the
other one. The Philadelphia job fell through; otherwise I'd be in
Philadelphia right now. But anyway, that job fell through, so I wrote
GSA and said "I'm going to graduate two months early and then I'll
come up," and they said "Come on."*

*So I started working for GSA as an engineer, and actually I be-
came a building inspector. During that time, I got into what I call a
training program, so I was able to move up pretty fast; I went from a
GS5 to a GS11 in about two years. That was something that was un-
precedented, especially for a black engineer. Then I wanted to go
from a GS11 to a GS12, and my white bosses said no, although my
white counterparts were getting similar promotions. So a number of
us took them to Capitol Hill through Congressman Adam Clayton
Powell, who had a subcommittee at that time. They put it in the
newspaper that a number of us took our bosses to the Hill, complaining that we could not get promoted. We also wanted to know
why they would not go to Howard University and train students.
They would instead go to Virginia Tech and all these other white
schools, and bring kids in and let them work during the summer. But
Howard University? Never. The story they gave was, "Well, they're
so close here, we want to bring people in from out of town."*

*Well, after we wrote that to Congressman Powell and he made a
famous speech here, the rules changed so that the next year or so
students from Howard University were able to come in and go to*

school. Many of those students are now doing great work, but they don't know of the effort made to clear the pathway for them.

Later, I got a job with the National Institute of Health, and I worked there several years before getting a job at the U.S. Navy Department. I worked there for about 15 years, designing generators for ships. In 1984, I handed in my resignation and I started working full-time with my brother Joe. I became top salesman for about eight years. I was the top salesperson in Dudley Products, Inc., because I was so determined.

During all of these years, I saved my money and bought real estate. I now own real estate valued at more than $1 million, because I saved and invested my money and didn't throw it away.

One day in 1988, I was at A & T State University, and I ran into a close friend. Let me back up for a minute. I had a friend at A & T who didn't live far from me, and I called him "Homie." His name is Alexander Gardner. We had an instructor in our first year at A & T who did not know basic electrical engineering. He just didn't know the subject matter. Can you imagine? Neither I nor the teacher knew anything. Fortunately, my friend did. He had studied electronics in the Army, so he tutored me. He helped me to get a fresh start. I'll always be indebted to him. He changed his major from electrical engineering to physics. He got a degree in physics, and I got my degree in electrical engineering. After graduation, I didn't hear from him anymore. After 30 years, I ran into Alexander Gardner at an A & T alumni meeting. He saw me and said, "Hi, Alfred." And I was looking at him, saying "I don't know who this is." When you haven't seen someone in 30 years, you picture in your mind how the person looked the last time you saw him. Now he's got all this gray hair and a beard, you know, but when he told me his name I could definitely see the resemblance. Boy, that was an exciting moment—to greet my old friend again.

I said "Gardner, I've told everybody how much you helped me."

Gardner said, "Well, guess what. I've told everybody how much you helped me."

I just knew he was being facetious, so I asked "Well, Gardner, what do you mean by that?"

Walk by Faith

He said, "You did help me."

"Wait a minute," I said. "You've got to explain."

"Okay," he told me. "When I left A & T, I taught for a couple of years, and then I went to the University of North Carolina to get my Ph.D. in Physics. When I went into class, I sat on the front row, and then everybody on the front row moved back. I was the only black man in class. They would write 'Nigger go home' on the blackboard."

He went on to say that A & T had academically prepared him for this the way my high school had prepared me for engineering. That is, we were not prepared. His classmates were from MIT and some other big schools, and they were well prepared to go on and get their doctorates, and he was not.

So Gardner said he started to leave, but then he thought about me. He said to himself, "Wait a minute; if Alfred Dudley could once overcome what he did, I can overcome this now." And he said that because of my work ethic and example he went on and finished, and was the first person, black or white to get a Ph.D. in four years, and graduate in the top of his class.

When he told me that, I tell you I was excited. Then he said, "I've told every class—and I've taught thousands of students—your story. I told them, 'You've got to have that work ethic like Alfred Dudley.' " I didn't know all those people had heard about my work ethic, and it made me feel excited that I had done something that possibly helped someone else—people I had never seen and would never see. I was shocked to learn that he had been right here at Howard University all these years. The head of the Physics Department, and I didn't know it. I have passed within, I would say, 500 feet of him probably hundreds of times and didn't know he was there. He had me to come in and speak to one of his classes, and boy that was an exciting moment. He kind of stretched the truth a little bit when introducing me. He said, "This is the man who's in charge of all of Dudley Products." But I had an exciting time there, and it was a lot of fun.

My life is proof that if you set goals for yourself, have faith, work hard, and have determination you can accomplish anything.

Flying With the Eagles

John Raye
Special Assistant to Mr. Dudley
and Senior Director of
Direct Sales

From the first time we met in Washington, D.C., in 1986, I knew Mr. Dudley was a special man. He has a spirit that is positive and dynamic. He is successful, but mindful of the road that led to that success. Mr. Dudley possesses something that sets him apart from the ordinary. He has an astonishing amount of faith about everything he does. He's a man very conscious of God's great potential to supply each of us a life of abundance.

My wife, Rosie, and I had been in business for ourselves for about 10 years. We had built up our business the old-fashioned way, by working sunrise to sunset and beyond. We had discovered, however, that hard work alone does not guarantee wealth and success. Despite the number of hours we put into our business, our financial situation was always strained. It seemed as if we were working just to keep up rather than to get ahead.

My friendship with Mr. Dudley grew strong, and the more time I spent with him, the more I learned. I credit Mr. Dudley with helping me to master self control and deal with anger, depression, and frustration. But, the most important thing that Mr. Dudley taught me was the results that were possible if I remained faithful.

My wife and I relocated to North Carolina from Washington, D.C., to work at Dudley Products. We had lost our retirement sav-

ings and were on the verge of losing our home and commercial building to foreclosure. I was in a state of deep depression when Mr. Dudley came to our aid. Not only did he pay the $370,000 mortgage on our property, but he also offered my family jobs in his company.

I cannot adequately express the gratitude I felt upon arriving in North Carolina. I looked up to Mr. Dudley. He took me under his wing, and each morning I would drive to his house and join him for a long walk. One day, while we walked through the newly developed subdivision in which the Dudleys lived, Mr. Dudley remarked about a lovely home being built just a few hundred feet from his own. He said, "John, it sure would be nice if you and Rosie lived in that house. Then you would not have to drive so far each morning for our walks."

I didn't respond, but I thought to myself, "Who does Mr. Dudley think I am? The price of the house has to be more than $700,000, and I certainly did not have that kind of money. Even in my wildest dreams, I could not imagine actually owning a house of that size. I was silent for the remainder of our walk. The next morning, Mr. Dudley again remarked that it would be nice if Rosie and I could live in that house. He said that people who knew about our turbulent past in Washington, D.C., could look to Rosie and me and see that it's possible to overcome even the toughest obstacles. Slowly but surely, I began to visualize my wife and me living there.

Over the next two months, Mr. Dudley, Dr. Bailey, and I walked and prayed that God would show Rosie and me how we could afford the house. We walked inside the frame of the house and prayed. I grew excited about the miracle I was expecting. Every day, rain or shine, we went to the house and prayed. We asked God to help us buy the house so that we could be an example to others of the miracles created by prayer, meditation, and sustained faith.

My mind would sometimes fall back on the fact that Rosie and I had less than $5,000 in cash and a combined income of only about $70,000 a year. But Mr. Dudley kept saying, "Do it by faith; not reason, John." I tried to follow his advice. When my reasoning led me to think about our other bills, my faith said don't worry. When rea-

son said that we could not afford furniture for the house, my faith said don't worry. When reason taunted me about our credit history, faith said don't worry. My faith grew strong.

From the moment we acted on faith and put a $5,000 deposit on the house, miracles started happening. We got an offer on our home in Washington, which had been on the market for months. With the proceeds from that sale, we were able to apply $200,000 more to the deposit. Then we signed the contract to purchase and went shopping for a mortgage lender. As a condition of our contract, we were informed that if we failed to find a lender within a year, we would lose our entire deposit. The thought of losing $205,000 made me sick in my stomach. But Mr. Dudley constantly reminded me that the opposite of fear is faith.

Within two months, another miracle occurred. We found a mortgage lender who took a chance on us. The lender financed the house for us with no co-signer. Hallelujah! The deal was signed, sealed, and delivered! Rosie and I moved into our new home in March 1995.

If I never see another miracle in this lifetime, I am satisfied that I witnessed this one first-hand. I am a strong believer in the power of prayer and the miracles that result from having just a little bit of faith. After coming so close to being destitute back in Washington, the idea of believing in faith that all things are possible was lost somewhere deep within me. But Mr. Dudley pulled it out again. I have renewed vigor and enthusiasm about each new day. I celebrate life with a passion that is relentless and rock-solid. I live each day by faith.

I thank God for Mr. Dudley, a mighty man whose life seems ordered by God. March on, Mr. Dudley. I am right behind you!

Change Your Attitude to Change Your Life

I learned at a young age that adversity makes you stronger. It builds character. Looking back on it, I realize just how easy it is to develop a negative mental picture of yourself when the only comments people make about you are negative. I also learned that having a negative perception of yourself leads to negative actions and undesirable results, because you become a product of your own thinking. And if you don't pull yourself out of a rut, life becomes one bad experience after another.

Lucky for me that I had someone who believed in me. My mother always told me that I could be anything I wanted. She helped me realize that it doesn't matter what other people think of me. All that matters is how I think of myself. So even now, when I get discouraged about something, I take a minute to think about what my mother used to say: "You can do anything, Joe, if you put your mind to it." I also read a lot, especially if I'm going through something important, or need to make a critical decision. I've found that reading gives me the wisdom and direction I need to clear my mind.

Walking is yet another remedy for me. I take long walks, sometimes by myself and sometimes with a group of people. I've discovered that walking, whether it's at dawn or in the cool of the evening, is quite comforting. As I walk, looking at nature around me, I realize just how small a part I play in the great scheme of things. Suddenly, the things that cause me stress seem so inconsequential. I have a lot to be grateful for. Being reminded that many people are struggling to get even their most basic needs met forces me to think twice about whatever circumstance is standing in the way of my focusing on more important goals.

Sometimes I repeat the Serenity Prayer: *Lord, give me the strength to accept the things that I cannot change, the courage to change the things I can, and the wisdom to know the difference.* Repeating self-affirmations can be really powerful. It helps to feed positive thoughts to your subconscious mind, which directs you to take positive actions. I often repeat to myself, *I am healthy, happy, wealthy, and wise,* and a great majority of the time it's true.

Another powerful affirmation I am used to is *I AM! I CAN! & I WILL!* I feel a surge of power rush through me when I say those words aloud. It makes me feel like yelling out "Watch out world, here I come! Move, mountains! Enemies, get under my foot! I am Joe Louis Dudley and *I AM! I CAN! & I WILL!*"

Great things happen when I start repeating those three simple lines. I get an attitude adjustment—a positive attitude adjustment.

If you don't believe me, try it the next time you're faced with a troubling situation. Go for a walk and have a little talk with yourself. Just keep repeating: *I AM! I CAN! & I WILL!* and put some feeling in it when you say it. The results will amaze you.

Make Your Own Break

Have you ever met someone who seems to have nothing but bad luck? The kind of person who seems to get out of one bad situation only to get stuck in the middle of another? It's like a never-ending cycle.

Well, I've met a few of these people. They're the sort of people who stumble through life always a day late and a dollar short. Always making do but never making any accomplishments.

I believe that 90% of the time, the reason behind this kind of misfortune is a bad attitude. They are thinking negatively about most people and every situation. Since they don't see the good in anything, they end up not trying, not dreaming, not really living. But there is hope. There is a way to change from seeing only big clouds of negativity to seeing nothing but rainbows and sunshine. It's as simple as making an attitude adjustment.

My good friend, the Reverend Jesse Jackson, is a living example of the way hope and determination can overcome what could be perceived as a negative situation. Young Jesse did not know his natural father for a number of years, but that did not deter him from dreaming, hoping, and achieving. His drive, plus the support and encouragement of his mother—an accomplished cosmetologist—led him to become one of the world's preeminent civil rights warriors, and the chief advocate of the "Keep Hope Alive" attitude.

The minute you catch yourself thinking a negative thought, stop; then focus on something nice. Talk about positive things and try to think positive thoughts. Repeat positive self-affirmations and associate with other positive-thinking people. Let their good energy rub off on you. Only by making a conscious decision to adjust your attitude can you ever attain wealth, success, or personal fulfillment.

Remember: the result you get from any situation depends largely on the thought you put into it. It takes a lot of positive energy to accomplish anything worthwhile. To grow a beautiful garden, you have to put some energy into pulling weeds, planting good seeds, and keeping the soil moist. The same thing applies to life. If you do nothing but sit around complaining and making excuses, then you will never achieve your dreams. It takes no energy whatsoever to grow weeds. Do nothing and you'll get nothing. It's just that simple.

Successful People Don't Make Excuses

One day several years ago, a good friend and I were sitting around talking. My friend told me that he could never get too far in business because he didn't have a college education. He said that not going to college was preventing him from being successful.

Frustrated by his negative thinking, I told him he was making excuses.

"There are plenty of rich and successful people who do not have college degrees," I pointed out. "Instead of creating alibis, they create opportunities for themselves."

I told him about S. B. Fuller, my personal mentor, who was a talented and very wealthy man. Mr. Fuller was able to build an empire even though he'd gone to school only three months a year before dropping out in the sixth grade. I turned to my friend and said, "Just think, if Mr. Fuller could become one of the wealthiest black people in America, despite lacking a formal education, then surely you can accomplish something, too."

I encouraged him to set his sights higher and do something more than making excuses. Fly high and the negative rats will drop off.

"Change your attitude," I told him. "Sure, getting an education is important; but if you don't, you won't be doomed for the rest of your life."

We grew up at a time when people could succeed in all kinds of businesses with little or no schooling. Anybody can learn skills and create opportunities to use those skills to their advantage. But one thing is for sure, I told him: "You've got to take action, and adjusting your attitude to think more positively is a good first step."

Almost half of all millionaires today are self-made. They are people who discovered ways to attain wealth, and worked hard to make it happen. They are living proof that business skills can be learned in the absence of formal education. Besides, once you become a millionaire, most people don't care about how much education you have. In fact, they are generally more intrigued by millionaires who've made it without formal education. Sheer determination and a positive attitude are the determining factors.

How else could someone with the obstacles and disadvantages that I faced so early in life have accomplished more than the very people who put me down? I'm here to tell you that it had less to do with what I learned in college than it did with on-the-job training under a caring mentor. Likewise, some of the most accomplished businessmen and salespeople I've ever known will tell you the same thing.

Study the Habits of Successful People

If you feel incapable of achieving wealth, success, and personal fulfillment on your own, I encourage you to seek out someone who has achieved the goals you aspire to and follow their example. Watch them. Study their work habits. Focus on the way they act and react in different situations and, most important, observe whether they think positively.

Do whatever it takes to convince yourself that you alone determine the boundaries and limits of your success. Remember: If you do nothing, that's exactly the result you'll get—nothing. You must believe that you can achieve anything. When you change your attitude, then you change your results. A positive attitude is the key to wealth, success, and personal fulfillment. So, dare to say *yes* to success.

Life Is No Problem

I have a life with no problems. I mean that. There is nothing that happens to me or around me that I would call a problem. I call the difficulties life presents *challenges*. Challenges can be overcome. Besides that, my mindset is completely different when I consider that I am being challenged as opposed to being burdened with problems.

Having a problem brings feelings of negativity. Problems make me feel miserable. I prefer to focus on the positive aspects of a bad situation. I try to look on the bright side and to see the opportunity that lies within every obstacle. Being challenged helps build strength, perseverance, and character.

There is a challenge involved in acquiring anything of value. But having a positive outlook is an important factor in finding true happiness. Focus only on the good things you want, and you won't have time to focus on the things you don't want.

That Good Ol' Dudley Spirit

In the street, in the crowd, in your home,
When you're all alone!
Highway, Byway, Highway Byway
You ought to take the Dudley Spirit, everywhere you go!
(Excerpt, company song)

As a company, we strive to help others achieve economic empowerment and self-sufficiency. We also work hard to educate others, especially young people. We try to be innovative and insightful in everything we do. To this end, we recognize our company as an industry *leader.* You'll never hear us slandering our competition. We can only compare our commitment to excellence and spirit of compassion to our past performance and future aspirations. Mr. S. B. Fuller always said, *"Only losers compare themselves to other people,"* and we certainly don't do that.

Observers on our campus or in our corporate office often comment on the positive atmosphere we have. We are happy. We are friendly. We are professional. We are motivated. Each of us has adopted and internalized the following principles in our lives:

- I am a valuable person. The direction I take in life is important; therefore, I value every decision I make.
- I accept prosperity and the abundance of life.
- I trust that everything comes at the perfect time and in the perfect day.
- I allow myself to think and dream in unlimited ways.
- All answers are within me. I choose to follow my inner vision and wisdom.
- I say "yes!" to success.

Dudley Products is made up of some of the most successful and talented people this country has to offer. We come from different walks of life. Some of us have been through some difficult times. Our backgrounds are not all without blemish. But today, we are all on a mission to achieve wealth, success and personal fulfillment.

There is a special spirit among the people at Dudley Products that makes us stand out from most other organizations. We are serious about self-improvement and empowering others. We are committed to having a life of abundance. We are excited beyond words about life and all of the opportunity that it offers. We have been conditioned to give up such words as *I can't* and *I won't* and to replace them with an attitude of *I AM! I CAN! & I WILL!*"

We strive to stir up everybody we come in contact with. We want them to share our excitement. We smile. We sing. We testify. We have been blessed in so many ways. We have learned to be optimistic and enthusiastic about our future. We all have caught the "Dudley spirit," and we carry it everywhere we go.

Happiness Is Helping Others

Motivating young people and challenging them to be more excited about life is one thing that our company strives to do. We established a corporate mentoring program for students at the James B. Dudley High School in Greensboro. Participants in this program must maintain a grade-point average of 3.0 and participate in a variety of company-sponsored programs on motivation and leadership. Our employees donate money each pay period to fund activities for the group. They also volunteer time to mentor the students in an effort to develop future business leaders.

In 1991, the Joe Dudley Fellows Program was honored by former President George Bush as the 467th "Daily Point of Light." After seeing the impact of our program on the participants, we formed the Eunice Dudley Ladies Program to foster personal development among high-school girls and to help them become women with self-confidence and academic excellence. Students in both programs are encouraged to be role models to their peers.

Dudley Products, Inc. was also presented the "Vision for Tomorrow" Award by the Direct Selling Association (DSA) for our outstanding community service efforts. This award recognized all the Dudley employees who voluntarily donated money each week to benefit such campaigns as:

- Our five-year, $250,000 commitment to the Adopt-A-School program with two local high schools.
- The $75,000 toward the renovation of Hayes-Taylor YMCA.
- The $10,000 donated for the East Forsyth Citizens for Human Services' Building Fund, Girl Scout Camp Keyauwee and for Bennett College, through the United Negro College Fund scholarship programs.
- National sponsorship of the Black Teen-age World Scholarship Pageant.
- Products delivered to our troops during the Persian Gulf War.

Realizing that only a tiny percentage of accountants in America are minorities, Dudley Products set out to change the statistics. With the aid of our employees, we initiated a program, COMPASS, for minority high-school students interested in careers in accounting. COMPASS offers seminars and classes to give these students the direction and hope they need if they are to carry out their ambitions. We help them obtain internships and form mentoring relationships with existing accountants.

All of our community activity is the result of our employees' initiative. Being **Dudley-rized** means having a spirit of compassion for others. We don't waste time on rhetoric. We take action. Being **Dudley-rized** means striving to help others achieve the same degree of wealth, success, and personal fulfillment that each of us aspires to. We want to make a difference in the world, and we all are committed to starting where we are with what we have. The Master said to cast your nets where you are.

First You Must Give to Succeed

Giving back—reaching out and helping others—will always be a top priority for us. We feel it is our duty and responsibility. We take this very seriously, and I try to play a role in dictating just how important giving back really is. Like most company presidents and self-made millionaires, I am constantly solicited to join boards of directors, civic organizations, and leadership programs. I recognize, however, that I cannot do all things and do them all well. So I am forced to choose carefully among the many offers I receive to participate. I seek out opportunities that put me in the company of people who are as committed to developing people as I am.

I joined DSA (Direct Selling Association) many years ago. The members of DSA shared both my background in sales and my vision to empower individuals through selling. I became chairperson of DSA's Inner City Task Force. My job was to seek out effective ways that DSA could give back to the community. One of our very first activities was to aid the victims of the Los Angeles riots after the Rodney King trial. We offered our technical expertise and business experience in an effort to serve as role models for inner-city residents of that area.

Our mission was to help the residents of Los Angeles to see that they could independently improve themselves. DSA member companies, such as Mary Kay Cosmetics, Tupperware, Amway, Shaklee Corporation, Princess House, Kitchen Fair, NuSkin International, Inc., The Longaberger Company and others, pooled resources to give these inner city residents tools for self-empowerment.

We donated thousands of dollars to the re-establishment of businesses and we also emphasized the importance of job creation. We gave many individuals the opportunity to work for our companies. We empowered them by offering sales positions that would make them job-makers instead of job-takers. The Los Angeles business community benefited from Dudley Cosmetology University's efforts as well. More than 3,400 alumni of the shool donated money to help the cosmetologists in that city rebuild their businesses.

Being a part of a group effort to effect change helps our company to accomplish much more than we would be able to do by acting alone. If you have bought into the concept of becoming wealthy, successful, and personally fulfilled, then I suggest that you get involved in your community.

You will reach a point in life at which money alone is not sufficient. Helping others, sensing how important your efforts are to them, and watching them become economically empowered and personally fulfilled is much more important. Giving back makes it all worthwhile.

Giving Back Bears Fruit

The Master said, "Go into my vineyard and work, and I will pay you."

Mrs. Dudley and I have received awards and honors from individuals and organizations nationwide. We gratefully display as many of these as space allows in the upper lobby of our corporate office. We know that regardless of how the inscriptions are stated, the awards are the result of having a strong, talented team of employees. It is because of the dedication and loyalty of our employees—many of whom have been with us from the time we first started out in business—that we have enjoyed building a company with 35 million in annual sales.

In July 1992, Mrs. Dudley was granted the prestigious Crystal Award by the Negro Business and Professional Women's Clubs, Inc. The Crystal Award, presented once a year at the organization's national convention, honors black women for their outstanding business accomplishments. Recipients are also judged on the basis of how well they uplift and improve the lives of other black women, both personally and professionally. Mrs. Dudley, through her dedication to the community, and through helping others to improve their lives, is the personification of this criterion.

In 1995, I was honored to receive the Horatio Alger Association of Distinguished Americans Award. Hundreds of nominations were received for this award, given annually to only ten individuals who have achieved success despite difficult childhood circumstances. Included in the lineup of individuals awarded with me were Quincy Jones, CEO of Quest Records; Don Shula, former head coach of the Miami Dolphins; and Jerry Dempsey, chairman and CEO of PPG Industries, among others. The Horatio Alger Awards Ceremony was nationally televised in a one-hour special.

I have identified only a few of the many awards we have received. I want to emphasize that we are not so concerned with the number of awards; rather, we hope our efforts will help youth to see that any challenge can be overcome through hard work, persistence, motivation, and determination. It is our goal at Dudley Products to help build a strong and safe future by serving as an example to many.

Times and Places

Stan Anderson
Former Dudley Route Sales Manager
New York City

*When I was a youngster growing up, I admired the lifestyles of
the gangsters in our neighborhood. Although my mother reared me
based upon Christian values, I was nonetheless enticed by the image
of the hustlers I saw wearing fancy clothes and driving sporty cars.*

*When I got old enough to understand a thing or two about the
streets, I began to lead a double life. In school and at home, I played
the role of a serious, clean-cut guy. But after hours, I was running
with the wrong crowd and working on my reputation as a gangster.
When I was 18 years old, I was arrested and convicted for robbery. I
served two years of a four-year sentence before being released into
a college program offered through the prison.*

*At the time, a friend of my family worked for Dudley Products as
a salesman and suggested that I could earn money for school by doing the same. He introduced me to Mr. Dudley, and from our first
meeting, I was intrigued by him. Mr. Dudley exemplified something
that I'd never seen much of: a successful brother on the right side of
the law.*

*As I talked with him, I was amazed that someone so successful
would spend even a few minutes getting to know me. Mr. Dudley
took a personal interest in my life and encouraged me to re-direct
my energy into something positive. He gave me a chance to work for
his company. He'd often pull me aside just to talk and counsel me.*

44

Change Your Attitude to Change Your Life

Mr. Dudley gave me the encouragement and inspiration I needed to turn my life around. After five years of door-to-door sales, I bought my first home. When I caught the Dudley spirit, I gained a lot of hope about my future. I believe for the first time in my life that I am, I can, and I will accomplish things on the positive side of the law. I've owned the clothes and cars that I used to fantasize about when I was younger. But I got them by working hard, changing my attitude and spirit, and living by faith—just as Mr. Dudley recommends. Following is a poem I wrote (while incarcerated) that has kept me focused and able to reach my goals:

Times and Places

Life is a series of times and places,
Of breathtaking advances and bitter retreats,
Of towering mountains, deep dark valleys,
victories, stalements and defeats.

Life is a journey that many will make,
but many will choose to stay home;
Some will set goals, reach them and stop;
Others will continue to forge on.

And don't we all have appointments that we should keep;
Don't we miss some, make some, sometimes oversleep;
But life is the total of our hits and our misses,
Of our sure things, our long shots, and our doubts;

And the thing we should be striving for
when our final score is taken
Is to have a high score that wins out.
For the clocks will keep ticking, the earth will keep turning,
The rivers will continue to flow;

But our lives are just a series of times and places,
And we all should choose someplace to go.
Don't spend your time dreaming or reminiscing,
Because there are places to go that you will surely be missing.

Don't cling to this earth because you are afraid to fly,
But spread out your wings and give life a try.

And should you start getting weary because your journey is long,

WALKING BY FAITH

Then call upon your mind to compose you a song,
And sing it wholeheartedly as you journey on.
Or stop and rest, but don't rest too long;
Don't quit your journey once you've begun,
But continue your struggle to the very end;

For you will be getting closer, yes you soon will be near it;
Near that horizon of hope that inspires your spirit.
Ignore the expressions of envious and doubtful faces,
And think only upon the days when there will be smiles and embraces;

And should you reach your destination
and find that you are not pleased with it,
Just rejoice in the fact that you made the trip,

And think of all the others who didn't even try;
Chances are the place they were born is the place they will die.
No, don't you ever think the journey you've made is a waste;
Just try another time and another place;
Another time, and another place!

—H. Stan Anderson
1980

NO TIME TO PLAY

My people have no time to play,
To flaunt around and while away!
Our tears and toils have just begun,
For we have a mighty race to run.
We must light the sparks of high resolve,
And climb the rugged hills of fame,
And with the nobles, write our name.

My people cannot whine and beg,
For dole and crumbs and daily bread,
If we hope to gain or win,
Complete respect of other men.
No, no, we have no time to play;
We must hurry forward while it's day.
With all our might we must fight to win,
And cling together to the end.

46

Change Your Attitude to Change Your Life

We must take this great conflict in stride.
But in our souls let truth abide!
For heed not to what others say.
For indeed we have no time to play.
The hills we must climb to find our God,
Are rugged all the way and hard!
But in order to make this journey pay,
We have no time to flaunt and play!

We have ten thousand things to do,
That call for grit, and faith anew,
That should be done, and must be done,
If this race is ever won!

We must build our factories and our banks,
We must toil as one, and close our ranks,
And show the world it can be done,
Through work and not by having fun.

Yes, my people, they must labor hard,
In answer to the will of God.
Toiling, struggling every day,
We never have time to play!

My people must join hand and heart,
And fight as one, and not fall apart.
It matters not what others say,
We do not have any time to play.

—The Reverend Richard Collins

Embracing the Dudley Spirit

Joanie Hayes
Director of International—Africa

*I officially joined Dudley Products, Inc. (DPI) in August 1980.
For two years before that, I sold products part-time while in college.
My affiliation with DPI started with acceptance of a "free" two-
week trip to Chicago.*

*July 21, 1980, was a very special day for me. It was my 21st
birthday, and I was ready to celebrate. During this stage of my life, I
was a very frustrated individual. I felt I always had to keep a certain
amount of excitement going in my life just to make it from one day to
the next. I had started experimenting with drugs and alcohol, and I
would open and close the dance floor any night of the week. So what
could I possibly do on "my special day," when there were few limitations?*

*My sister and a couple of friends decided to take me shopping in
Winston-Salem, N.C. You can't plan to party and celebrate without a
new "hip outfit." We drove to Winston-Salem, picked up a bag of
marijuana, and started a day that would change my life forever.*

*Before going to the mall, I suggested that we stop at The Dudley
Beauty Center on Liberty Street to speak to one of my favorite
cousins, Sheila Hayes. She was always a person I admired because
of her determination and her love for life after her battle with
cancer.*

Change Your Attitude to Change Your Life

When I entered the building, there were four or five well-dressed men, all in dark suits, standing at the counter. As I proceeded to the counter, I was informed that Sheila was not in; she was in Chicago. As I exited the salon, one of the gentlemen struck up a conversation. He didn't introduce himself, but was very inquisitive about what type of employment I had, where I was attending college, what my favorite subject was, and what my plans were for the future. I could answer all the questions from the tip of my tongue, except for the last one. I really hadn't given too much thought concerning life after college. I only knew I wanted to find a good job that paid well. We spoke only briefly, and as I was leaving he said, "When you finish college, you should come to Chicago with Sheila and set some real goals for your life."

An indescribable feeling seemed to engulf my every thought from the moment I left the premises. I no longer had thoughts of celebrating my birthday; instead, there were thoughts of my future.

Two weeks later, Sheila drove from Chicago to my parents' home. She said she had come to take me to Chicago for two weeks. It sounded exciting, but I had many reasons to feel I shouldn't go. In three weeks it would be time for me to go back to college for my last semester. I wanted to spend time with my son before leaving. My family was planning our annual trip to the beach, and I had invited some classmates from college. But regardless of the excuse I gave Sheila, she had an answer. I remember her saying, "It'll be so nice when you go back to college and tell everyone you had the opportunity to go to Chicago, the Windy City, for your summer break." The more she talked, the better it sounded. So I agreed.

My First Dudley Sales Meeting

We arrived at the sales meeting early and refreshed. When the meeting started, I was totally amazed. It was 8 o'clock in the morning, and the people were singing and dancing around as if they were at a party. They sang songs about making money, buying cars, living on Park Avenue, and yes, they even sang about owning diamonds, furs, and yachts. Now when I arrived in Chicago, I didn't take any drugs or artificial stimulants with me. I had plans to find the "good stuff" and take it back to North Carolina. When I saw all this energy and enthusiasm flowing so early in the morning, I just knew the salespeople had to be high on something.

There was one common ground that they all spoke about, which really got my attention. They spoke of their gratitude to God for their opportunity to be a part of Dudley Products Company and the privilege to work for such a man as Mr. Joe L. Dudley, Sr.

Now I had sold the products on a very small scale years previously, and had always heard Sheila speak of her boss. But I had not knowingly met this "superstar" of a man. I had always assumed that Mr. Dudley was some gray-haired, retired little man, sitting back enjoying his riches. The manager announced that Mr. Dudley had just arrived in front of the building. Now the spirit in the room was really high.

Everyone stood and clapped for the welcoming of "the boss." I was totally shocked to find this man to be the same gentleman I had met at the Dudley Beauty Center just two weeks earlier. This was the man who spoke only brief words, but with so much depth, that it made me stop for the first time in my life and give serious thoughts about my future.

This man spoke with deep conviction about the power each of us possessed. It was like being hypnotized. That day, I knew my life would never be the same.

After the meeting, several people awaited the opportunity to speak with Mr. Dudley in a back room behind the meeting area. It wasn't even set up as a proper office, but the people waited patiently. Before Mr. Dudley left, he greeted me and said he was happy I had made the trip. I later went into the field with Sheila, meeting all her customers as she made sales.

We talked the whole day about DPI and its people. I was amazed to learn of the various backgrounds of the employees. More than half of the top sales people had overcome severe challenges in *life, including drug addiction, alcoholism, attempted suicide, and even incarceration. It was on the second day that I had the opportunity to speak to Mr. Dudley personally. After the morning meeting, Mr. Dudley asked me to come to the back office.*

The conversation began with a series of questions similar to those at our first meeting. He kept asking me what was I living for and what I wanted out of life. He asked whether I had a plan to reach my goals. I had to say "not really." Then the big question was asked: "Are you on any type of drugs or artificial stimulant?"

The question caught me by surprise, but something compelled me to be truthful.

"Why would this man, a stranger, ask me such a personal question?" I wondered.

Very few people knew of this darker side of my life. My parents, relatives, and college associates didn't know of my drug usage. I had been reared in a rather sheltered Christian home, where certain actions were just not acceptable. But for the past year to 18 months I had become very frustrated with life, and nothing really seemed to matter anymore.

Before I could even answer Mr. Dudley's question, he said, "Great joy or great sadness cannot be hidden; I have worked with people for so many years and I can see that you are a very frustrated young lady."

And he was right. I replied that yes, I did smoke pot every now and then, but didn't care much for drinking. I told him I knew it wasn't right, and I had tried many times to stop, but I always ended up going back.

His next response changed my life forever. In a very piercing and powerful tone, Mr. Dudley demanded: "Why are you walking around like an accident in this world? You're made in the image of God. You could have been a dog, a cat, or a roach, but you're made in His image. You need to make something out of your life. You don't need dope; all you need is hope for the future."

That was the turning point in my life. Even during my frustrations, I would always pray to the Lord to help me get through these challenging times. I didn't know how or when it would happen, but I never felt forsaken. As Mr. Dudley spoke to me, I knew my prayers had been answered. He said if I would acquaint myself with God, commit myself to work, read self-help books, and follow the instructions of successful people, he would share with me the way to regain happiness and success in life.

I thank God that I took Mr. Dudley's offer. My life has not been the same since I joined DPI. There are so many experiences that I would love to share, because some of them might help to change someone's life. When I heard others share some of their innermost challenges in life and saw how they survived, I knew there was hope for me, because I changed my attitude and spirit.

"Life in the Big House"

After my first three or four days in Chicago, I was moved into a company-owned place called "The Big House." This appeared to be the starting point for most of the employees while they are awaiting steady income in sales. The house had five or six bedrooms and two bathrooms, and accommodated around 25 people at times. I slept in the "would be" living room with five other ladies and a small child. Some slept in chairs pulled together as beds, while others slept on couches or cot-beds. It would be an understatement to say that the living conditions were not the best.

Even though the overseers of the house tried to make everyone comfortable, the house was badly infested with roaches and mice. It may have been because of its location. There were several abandoned shacks nearby that needed to be torn down, as well as unmaintained lots that appeared to be havens for rodents. After almost three months of trying to stay positive and looking at the living situation as temporary, I'd had enough.

I was always afraid to sleep in the dark, so I kept a small night light plugged into the wall. On this particular night, after reading and preparing for tomorrow, everyone fell off to sleep. Since there were only two bathrooms, I would take my bath late at night and be the last one in the room. I was so used to staying up late at night partying that it was quite difficult to retire before 1 a.m. any night. After saying my prayers, I prepared myself for a peaceful night of rest. As I was drifting off to sleep, I heard a strange sound of paper being shuffled. I got up and turned on the lights. The sound stopped. I waited a couple of minutes before returning to bed. Just as I was drifting off again, the noise started very loud. I knew something was in the room. I jumped up screaming, turned on the lights and, of course, everyone woke up fussing.

I was standing on the bed while they ran to get the overseer of the house. He came in with a broom and said I was probably hearing things. As he took the broom handle to check under the tables, chairs, and beds, he pulled the shoes and my purse from under my bed. When he did, a huge black rat—not a mouse—came slowly crawling out. We all screamed and ran for safety. That rat was moving slowly because it had probably eaten some of the poison laid out for the mice. Eventually, the overseer killed the rat and took it out. It just didn't seem to want to die.

That was it. I'd had enough of Chicago and these living standards. I was packing my bags to go back to North Carolina. I called Mr. Dudley, in a rage, at 2:30 in the morning to tell him about the rat. I told him I had tried to follow his success program, but I couldn't live like this. I was hysterical. Mr. Dudley was very calm, and said it was fine if I wanted to leave. He said for me to be at the meeting in the morning and he would make arrangements for me to leave. I stayed up the rest of the night packing and preparing to leave.

The next morning I went to the meeting. Mr. Dudley came in and started his meeting as usual. Just as he started his closing remarks, he asked me to come up. I thought I was prepared for whatever he had to say, because I had a just reason to leave. As I arrived at the front of the room, Mr. Dudley informed the group that I would be returning to North Carolina.

Then he began to laugh. I didn't understand his laughter. He then apologized and said, "You really had me fooled. I really thought you were going to make it. But you are going to let a little rat keep you poor all your life. A little rat is going to run you all the way back to North Carolina." Again he started to laugh. This time all the salespeople joined in. Every time he would say the word "rat" everyone would laugh.

After a moment, I began to feel embarrassment—not because the group was laughing, but because it was true. I was leaving the big state of Illinois because of a rat, a rodent. Mr. Dudley composed himself long enough to say that some people let anything come between them and success, but in all his days he had never heard of a nasty little four-legged creature stopping anyone from succeeding. He said I was allowing that dead rat to have more sense than I.

Mr. Dudley really has a way of making you look for the good in every situation. He said that rat should not force me to give up on succeeding, but should inspire me to get my sales up, so I could move to a better location. And that is what I did. I sold products as I had never done before. My income skyrocketed. The next month, Sheila and I moved into a beautiful luxury condominium on Lake Shore Drive. It was on the Gold Coast, one of the richest areas of Chicago. I learned two important things: How much I could take before giving up, and what was stopping me from succeeding.

Riding By Faith

Originally, when I went to Chicago, I thought it would be only for two weeks. I had a car in North Carolina, but Mr. Dudley said since it was an old car I shouldn't go get it. He said I needed to start thinking like a successful person. Successful people don't drive around in old cars. So for more than a year, I got rides to the meetings, got dropped off in my territory, caught the bus and rode the "El." This took quite a bit of adjusting, because I had owned a car since I was 15. My dad owned a used-car lot, so vehicles were always plentiful at our home.

Change Your Attitude to Change Your Life

One day in the meeting, Mr. Dudley told a couple of us he wanted us to go to North Carolina to buy new cars. I was once again excited. I had so much belief in the fact that Mr. Dudley said I would get a new car that I forgot I didn't have money for the down payment. I didn't know where I would get the money or how, but I knew I would be the owner of a new car that chimed when you opened the door. That was my goal.

I called my father before I left Illinois so he could begin to scout for me. Once I arrived, we spent the first three days just looking at cars. I was being so choosy. The color had to be right. The seats had to be plush and sit a certain way. I wanted a certain type of stereo system. And of course the car had to have that special type of chime that was music to my ears. On the fourth day, I found the car of my dreams. It had everything that I wanted. When my dad saw that I had made a decision, he asked me how much money I had to work with so he could try to work out a deal with the dealer. I replied "I've only got $40, but that's my car."

With a very confused look on his face, he turned and asked the question again. My reply was the same. At this time, I think my father thought I had completely lost my mind. He drove home in silence as I chanted about my new car. Mr. Dudley had said for me to call once I had found the car, and the next program would be getting the money. When I called, he told me to get a sheet of paper and pencil right then, so I did. He told me to write down the names of the first ten people who came to mind. As he was talking, I began to write. Then he said once I completed the list I should ask each person to lend me $100.

I was already on my sixth name when he told me the purpose of the list. I stopped and said that I needed to change my list, because some of these people I know don't have the money and others I wouldn't want them to know that I was in need of financial help. He told me I had to get my pride out of the way if I wanted God to bless me. The car had to be the most important thing on my mind, and I shouldn't worry whether people would talk about me or not. The third name on the list was my brother Scottie. He was several years *younger than I, still in high school, and working only a part-time job. But I always felt he should have some money, because he was always so tight with cash. If he gave you a quarter, he would have to know when you would pay it back. Money was always very serious to him. I only hoped he had $100 to lend; I didn't even know whether he had a savings account.*

When I approached my brother, I told him what I was trying to do. I told him he was the third person on my list, and I was really counting on him to help. He shocked me. He said yes he had the money, and as a matter of fact he had $500 if I wanted to borrow it. Now that was a miracle in itself. By the time I got to my fifth name, I had more than enough money to get my car. I even paid my insurance for the full year. The lesson I learned was to believe that you have already received whatever it is that you asked for. You must walk by faith; anyone could have been excited if the money was in hand. But how is your faith when your back is pushed against the wall?

Listen and Read to Succeed

Find an Author, Find a Philosophy, and Practice It Until You Succeed

One of my favorite books is *Think and Grow Rich,* by Napoleon Hill. It took Hill more than 20 years to write this book, and it remains one of the greatest and most influential books ever written on attaining wealth and success.

Countless millions of copies have been sold, and to this day it is a perennial best seller. Reading *Think and Grow Rich* gave me a new sense of direction. It changed my life.

Napoleon Hill had a rather keen interest in the lives of successful people. More important, he wanted to know why, despite all the effort put forth, some people attained wealth and success, while others did not. He focused his investigation on the winners. He studied their positive experiences and took notes on how they achieved success.

Hill analyzed the habits of some of the richest and most successful people in America. He conducted personal interviews with such people as Thomas Edison, John D. Rockefeller, Andrew Carnegie and Franklin Roosevelt. He discovered that all his interviewees had certain traits in common, and in his book, he revealed the key common threads.

I like *Think and Grow Rich* so much because it makes sense. I can read the book and follow its guidance. I don't have to reinvent the wheel. I just follow what has already been proved to work. I pick it up and read it for a refresher several times every year. It's packed with logic that I never want to forget. In fact, I keep several copies of the book around my office so that I never miss a chance to share it with others.

Reading Stimulates Imagination

Reading is a big part of my life, even now. I want you to know just how important it is to read. Reading exercises the mind. It stimulates the imagination and gives you achievement drive. There is a world of opportunity available to anyone, but you first have to know that it exists. Reading will give you this awareness.

I am thankful to God for helping me to realize the importance of reading. About a year before I started to write this book, I took a look at my life, the company, and our employees, and decided that I needed to do more than I was currently doing to motivate and lead. I thought, "God had put us here for a limited amount of time, and we should make better use of the time he has given us."

We had actually grown complacent with the daily routine and knew that there must be some way to improve ourselves and help ourselves and the company achieve goals. I was searching for an effective way to motivate myself and our employees to achieve more by communicating more and working together with one accord.

Not knowing what else to do, I picked up my copy of *Think and Grow Rich* and studied it. In fact, for six straight hours I sat poring over the information. As a result of this quiet reading time, I was inspired to put myself on a ten-day program. I wrote out my plan of action. I challenged myself to get up each morning at 5 a.m. to read for two hours.

I don't mind telling you that it was tough at first; very tough. I had developed a habit of getting up in the middle of the night and sneaking a few cookies from the kitchen. But I made up my mind that I would abandon this habit for ten days. I had to pull myself out of bed each morning without anticipating an eye-opening cup of coffee, which I also gave up. Only for ten days, I reminded myself each morning. I can do this, I said. I have to take it one day at a time.

When ten days had passed and I had reached my goal, I added ten more days. I kept on adding days, reaching one goal and setting another. Eventually, my mind and my body got used to the changes I had made. I didn't miss the coffee or the cookies. I also came to love the solitude and peace that surrounded me each morning when I read. With each day, it became easier to get up at 5 a.m. and read.

Dudley's Daily Reading Program

The key is that I had to start somewhere. That's why I set the goal for ten days. Continuing beyond my initial goal was a cinch. I challenged myself to see just how long I could keep it up. And now, several years later, I'm still enjoying success. When I told a few Dudley's employees about my new regimen, many of them agreed to try it too. By far, the most positive result of sharing my experiences with my employees is the morning reading group we formed. We all agreed to meet at our corporate office each morning and have a 30- to 45-minute silent reading time, followed by a group discussion on the material we'd read. All participants are free to discuss what they've learned from the reading and how they can benefit from it. Our discussions are candid, invigorating, and sometimes quite heated.

We are learning more about ourselves, our motivation, and our potential for success. We read books about motivation and self-improvement. We are committed to bettering ourselves. Several of the books we've read and recommend to you are listed in the Appendix.

As an extension of our morning reading class, we began to have a longer reading session once a month. During these sessions, we read for six hours straight. It is the longest uninterrupted time most of us have ever devoted to concentrated reading. We chose the six-hour time period, believing that six hours is about how long it takes for an idea to have its full impact on the subconscious mind. We want our reading to make a permanent, lasting impression. We are committed to self-improvement and personal empowerment, and we believe that reading is the key to achieving it.

Our morning reading group meets absolutely every day—including weekends and holidays—without fail. Some people make one- to two-hour commutes each morning to participate. Obviously, they get something out of our reading. Many of our route sales managers follow our reading regimen from their homes. Some have formed little reading groups of their own, while others enjoy the opportunity to read in solitude every morning.

What's most amazing about our group readings is that it is a voluntary effort. The people who participate in the morning readings are motivated, and determined to make a difference in the world. Our reading group is full of people who think positively. We are all on a mission to better our lives and find wealth, success, and personal fulfillment. We each set goals every month and post them on the wall. Each morning, we mark off the goals that we've accomplished. We give encouragement and praise to one another.

One young man, Patrick Hill, joined our reading group shortly after enrolling at Dudley Cosmetology University. He lived in an apartment several miles from the corporate office. He knew that he was faced with a challenge one morning when his car wouldn't start. Unable to jump-start it or hitch a ride, Patrick made a quick decision. He walked. Despite the early morning frost, Patrick set out on foot with his book tucked under his coat. He made the trip each day on time. Patrick had made a commitment to the group—that he would be present every day, without excuse.

When I asked Patrick why he didn't call someone from the group to give him a ride, he told me that he didn't have anyone's telephone number. Well, we changed that right away. But there was no changing the fact that everyone in our group was impressed that Patrick refused to let a lack of transportation create an excuse for him to break a promise.

Patrick has since graduated and received his cosmetology license. He owns a salon in the community where he grew up, and he has employed a number of people from his neighborhood. He has accomplished a lot for a 21-year-old. Patrick knows that there is no substitute for success, and he has learned to deal with obstacles as they arise. I'd like to think that some of that ability arose from his experience with our morning reading group.

Reading on the Road

Even when we travel, it's not uncommon for our group to meet in a hotel lobby, restaurant or other designated space. We refuse to be deterred by the environment. We meet wherever space permits. After all, our spirits are not to be restricted by time, circumstance, or space.

I am very excited about our morning reading program. I have been enriched in all areas of my life by the things that I have learned through our readings and discussions. The more I learn, the greater my yearnings for new knowledge, information, and ideas.

As I remind my employees, it is only through reading that I have learned to maintain an employee base of more than 500 productive, satisfied people. I have also learned to meet a $50,000-a-day payroll. But most important, I learned how to turn a $10 investment into a multimillion-dollar business enterprise.

Now, I don't know everything, but I do know enough to build a brand new hotel from the ground up and an 80,000-square-foot manufacturing center. Reading opened the doors of my imagination and made it possible for me even to consider expanding our company into the international arena.

I don't recount these things with any measure of smug pride, but rather with extreme gratitude to God for helping me to realize the importance of reading and learning. Take advantage of the opportunity to read as often as you can. Commit to a daily reading program. In fact, join us in spirit tomorrow from wherever you are. You are certainly invited!

At the time of this writing, we are reading Stephen R. Covey's *The 7 Habits of Highly Effective People.* We will be reading it for at least six months to grasp the full benefit of its text.

Choose a Good Mentor
and Role Model

A Mentor's Influence

Mr. S. B. Fuller was my mentor and one of the fathers of modern day black businesses.

I believe that everybody can learn from the examples of others. Most people who have become successful in life had someone whom they patterned their lives after—someone whose lifestyle excited them. A mentor. This worked for me as well. Mr. Fuller was successful in life. He was one of the wealthiest black men in the United States. He was a self-made millionaire. He was a giant in the world of black hair-care and beauty aids. I learned tremendously from his example.

Mr. Fuller believed that through hard work any obstacle could be overcome. I appreciated hearing that. It reinforced my notion that I could overcome the characterizations that plagued my childhood. I didn't have to be mentally retarded. I didn't have to be slow. I didn't have to let a speech impediment stop me from speaking in public. The world had no limit as long as I worked hard.

Under Mr. Fuller's wise direction, I grew both personally and professionally. He was good at giving hope and encouragement. One of the many principles he shared with me was that "Every person is born with a spark of divinity, but it's up to the individual to fan that spark."

I understood that concept, and it became an important factor in my own teaching.

Mr. Fuller also believed in discipline, orderliness, courtesy, cleanliness, humility, and hard work. He taught all his employees that the answer to so many of our problems is grounded in economics. He constantly pushed us to "become job-makers and not job-takers."

He challenged us to believe in ourselves and the abilities we possessed. He chastised us whenever we failed to exercise our God-given potential. And, unlike many other self-proclaimed role models, Mr. Fuller practiced what he preached.

I cannot give Mr. Fuller enough credit for what he has meant to my life. Today, I continue to build upon the foundation he laid down years ago. I am grateful for the opportunity to have been among the many lives that he touched, influenced, and directed along the path of achievement.

The Importance of Role Models

Our nation, and the black race especially, needs more role models. We need people who are influential, effective leaders. There are too many people claiming to be leaders, but whose actions and results contradict their claims. Actions and results are the tell-tale—the bottom line when it comes to effectiveness as a role model.

Role models are creators of jobs and opportunities. People constantly seek them out. Role models are goal-oriented. They envision goals and refuse to let any obstacles get in the way of achieving them. They see an opportunity for greater accomplishment in every obstacle they encounter, and they remain focused on achieving success.

Role models do not get caught up with the way people feel about them. Their self-images are intact, and they have a tremendous amount of self-respect. Role models are energized persons who enjoy their journeys through life. Mr. Fuller exemplified all of these qualities, and I wanted to do the same thing.

Mr. Fuller's devotion to raising people reminds me a lot of the commitment Nelson Mandela has to the same goal. President Mandela has such overwhelming compassion for human life that he took on the cause of thousands of people in his native land of South Africa. He led the way. Mr. Mandela did not seek to make life better for himself alone; he desired to save an entire race of people. He sparked that flame of divinity within him and believed that anything was possible. Then he made it his personal goal to end apartheid.

Long before his efforts landed him in prison, he fought while in hiding or on the run. He had a cause, and made great strides to see it fulfilled. Even from within the walls of prison, Mandela saw more opportunity. Rather than quit and bide his time behind bars, he continued to devise plans for bringing about freedom from apartheid.

How many people do you know who would go to such an extreme? How many people do you know who could endure being in prison for trying to make their country a better place?

The Bible encourages us all to be more righteous. A righteous person cannot stand to witness wrongdoing, hurt, and suffering. It pains him so much that he becomes committed to take action. Mandela is a righteous man, and while the situation looked bleak for him at one point, just look at him now. He is a president, hero, and role model to people all over the world.

In my opinion, a righteous person lives by the Master's standards, not by man's standards. Most people live by man's standards and have set their standards too low. To be righteous is to follow the Master's example.

Qualities of Leadership

There are a few unchanging requisites that go along with effective leadership. As trends change and leaders come and go, the characteristics of effective leaders remain the same. We impress the following principles upon all of our sales managers and employees:

(1) **Initiative:** an internal drive to make things happen. People with initiative go beyond the call of duty to get things done; to

attain the things they want. Whether it's jobs, cars, houses, or whatever, people with initiative refuse to take no for an answer. They are creative about finding whatever resources they need to get the things they want. It's commonplace for people with initiative to hear such comments as "That person is a real go-getter," or "You're a lucky person; you always seem to get what you want." The truth of the matter is that luck has nothing to do with it. People with real initiative create their own luck.

Imagination is the creative faculty that drives *Initiative.* "Imagination rules the world," said Napoleon Bonaparte. It certainly does. It creates your vision, helps you develop goals and dreams, then gives you the way to achieve them. But you can achieve them only if you take action to achieve them. This action includes daring to do things without being told to do them. You adapt your sales talk to varying conditions, take time to evaluate a customer's buying patterns; a customer's needs. In short, you do without being told. This is *Initiative!* This is what leaders possess.

(2) **Courage:** the ability to face difficult situations. Real courage involves picking your fights carefully. Courage, as the country hit song reminds us, consists of knowing when to walk away and knowing when to run. In the face of adversity, people with courage don't shy away. They understand that personal challenges are going to come, because challenges are a part of life. But rather than be defeated by circumstances, they rise to the occasion and meet the challenge head-on. No situation is impossible to overcome for a person with courage.

At Dudley Products, I teach that *fear* is an *attitude of mind,* which asserts itself only when you let it. It is your thought about a thing that you fear, and not the thing itself. I encourage as many of our people as possible to do door-to-door selling, because this is an excellent way to overcome fear and develop the courage they need to become successful. Once the fear of failure is conquered and the ability to handle rejection is developed, they are well on their way to achieving their goals and dreams.

(3) **Loyalty:** being true to oneself and to the principles and people you believe in. You've heard the cliché, "Stand for something or fall for anything." This sums up loyalty. Loyal people are believers in what they do, the products they sell, the quality of services they offer, the principles they stand behind. Particularly from the viewpoint of a salesperson, you cannot successfully sell a product that you don't believe in. There is no place at Dudley Products for salespeople who market our products by day and use the products of our competitors by night. Being loyal means walking the talk. Loyalty is critical to the success of any leader.

We strongly believe that a loyal employee or salesperson does not make negative statements or remarks about the company or its products. This does not mean that they should blindly follow policies and sell products they know are substandard. It means that the employee or sales manager will not lie about the policies or products, but instead, will step forward and bring them to the attention of the company. Loyalty is not keeping silent when things go wrong; it is stepping forward to help make things right.

Let me give you an example of how challenging loyalty can be sometimes. Let's say you have a really close friend. You find out that this friend has done a tremendous injustice to someone. In fact, you know all the details. Because you know all the details, you also are in a position to right the wrong your friend has caused. To do so, you'll have to expose your friend. If you right the wrong, you will lose your friend. If you defend your friend or remain silent, you lose your own self respect and violate your sense of right.

In the end, we should follow the words of Shakespeare and "To thine own self be true." In other words, when conflicting loyalties surface, always be true to the real you and the side that represents the "true you."

(4) Integrity: a high level of moral character; honesty. People of integrity are unwavering in principle and moral standing. They are both value-driven and dependable. These are people you can count on. People of integrity require very little supervision. You can trust them to get a thing done; to stick with it until it's completed. Integrity is evident in people who say: "If my name or reputation is on the line, then everything is going to be done right."

Some people may be long on reliability but short on integrity. You might be able to trust them with your money and your products, but unable to trust them to look after your interests or customers. An example is a sales manager who calls on and services only the best prospects in his assigned area. While he may not take the company's money or waste the product inventory, he is guilty of robbing other customers of service and the company of potential business. A person of integrity can be counted on to do the complete job without direct supervision, and without short-changing anyone.

(5) Wisdom: the ability to create. Wisdom comes from God. Much like insight, wisdom cannot be taught, but it can be further developed once the gift of wisdom is first acknowledged. Wisdom is gained by looking up—not down.

Many confuse knowledge with wisdom. Unfortunately, many people have accumulated a great amount of knowledge that is of no value whatever. They have simply loaded their minds with an enormous amount of information (by looking down into books). They are not acting properly on the knowledge that will make them successful and happy.

The quality that uses this knowledge properly is wisdom, and wisdom comes when you listen to the voice within (by looking up to God) and discover your purpose in life. When this happens, it is amazing how knowledge and information take on a totally new importance. We see things differently, act differently, and achieve different things when we listen to God and accept his gift of wisdom.

Begin by asking God to show you his purpose for your life. Then step out in faith, and the knowledge and wisdom will follow.

Rough Nursing

I believe that before God bestows real nobility on you, He gives you a little "rough nursing" as a way of preparing you for it. By this I mean that when faced with all sorts of obstacles and challenges, we must overcome as a test of faith. Rough nursing is necessary for building endurance and strength. It is also an important element in developing humility and gratitude. Some people, including me, consider door-to-door selling a way of being nursed rough. This experience really puts you in touch with your true self. You learn something about your self-worth and your value system. It builds character, endurance, and self-confidence. It promotes courage, and is definitely a way of learning patience. When you master door-to-door selling, you have mastered training in developing a strong character.

Rough nursing existed even in Biblical years. One of the greatest stories on rough nursing is found in the Book of Job in the Bible. Job was a great man who was nursed rough. For years he was wealthy, healthy, and wise. He was blessed with a loving family, devoted friends, and an impressive list of material possessions. But before real nobility was bestowed upon Job, he lost everything.

Job lost his land and every one of his possessions. He lost his handsome face to many blisters and open sores. His friends accused him of having committed some great sin that resulted in what they believed to be punishment from God. Even his wife threatened to leave him. Although Job didn't understand why he was being so harshly tested, there was nothing he could do to end it. He endured all of the negative accusations and remained focused on serving God. His righteousness sustained him. Eventually, Job's body was physically restored, and he was blessed with three times as much as he had lost.

As you look through history, you will discover that the great mentors and leaders of our time have all endured obstacles and suffering. Behind every real hero there seems to be some tragic flaw, some test of faith. I call it rough nursing, for it is God's way of separating the men from the boys, and the women from the girls.

Mrs. Lestine Thornton Fuller

Wife of S. B. Fuller

I got to know my late husband, S B. Fuller, the same way that most people met him: on the job. From the first time I met Mr. Fuller, I determined that he was a hard-working person, never content with sitting around. He always needed to be doing something, and in sales, he found a perfect niche. Mr. Fuller believed that he was not put on this earth to be poor. His mother reared him to believe that poverty is not a permanent condition, and being born poor doesn't mean that you will end up that way.

Mr. Fuller recruited me to come to work for an insurance company in Chicago. I was just out of high school and wasn't very sure about whether I would go to college. My family was urging me to move to Washington, D.C, where my older sister could look after me and, they hoped, talk me into enrolling at Howard University, but I didn't want to do that.

*No sooner was I hired at the insurance company than Mr. Fuller decided that he was leaving that job. He wanted to go into business for himself, and he offered me the chance to join him. For the next 12 years, Mr. Fuller and I sold soap. He would buy discarded soap from big companies and bring it to our office, where I would spend day after day scrubbing off the name of the soap and cleaning it up to look as good as new. I would etch in the name **Fuller,** and Mr. Fuller would sell the soap door to door by day. There were times*

71

when business was slow and he couldn't afford to pay me very much, but I didn't mind. I was content just working alongside Mr. Fuller and hearing about all of his dreams and plans for the future.

When Mr. Fuller learned that one of the companies that supplied him soap was going to be sold at an auction, he started talking non-stop about buying it. I invested all the money I had saved to help him, and I begged for help from my friends and family as well. We had raised about $25,000, but we were still far from having enough money. Mr. Fuller put up the money we had and promised to pay the remaining $125,000 within ten days.

The terms of the agreement stated that if the balance wasn't paid within that time, he'd lose the $25,000 deposit. Anxious but determined, Mr. Fuller buckled down. He started calling everybody he knew, including our soap customers. For the next week, he busied himself doing nothing but raising money. As the tenth day drew near, Mr. Fuller had a total of $115,000. But, he still needed $10,000 more. With so little time left, he couldn't think of anyone else to ask for help. But, before he threw in the towel and faced the disappointment and the humiliation of defeat, Mr. Fuller got down on his knees and prayed. Humbly, he asked God for help.

After another day of knocking on doors, Mr. Fuller was tired. As he drove toward home, a small, still light in front of the office on 61st Street caught his eye. He was prompted to park his car and go into the office. The sign indicated that it was a contractor's office. When Mr. Fuller entered the office, he discovered that he knew the man working there. This being no time for small talk, Mr. Fuller looked at the man, who appeared somewhat tired, and got right to the point. He asked the man, "How would you like to make $1,000?"

"Why, of course, I would like that," the man answered.

"If you will make out a check for $10,000 to help me out," Mr. Fuller continued, "when I repay you the money—and I promise to repay you—I will give you $1,000 in interest."

The man was silent. He studied Mr. Fuller's eyes, probably trying to figure out whether he was crazy. Mr. Fuller broke the silence by explaining his dilemma in more detail. He offered the names of other people who had already agreed to help. After hearing Mr. Fuller's story, the man just smiled. He wrote out the check and handed it to him. From there, Fuller Products was born, and Mr. Fuller was on his way to achieving his dream of becoming rich.

Mr. Fuller and I got married, and I worked by his side to build our new company. By 1963, we had a sales force of more than 5,000 people and more than 100 items in the Fuller Products line. Fuller Products was the largest black-owned company in America. My husband eventually retired me from the business, encouraging me to travel and do other things I enjoy. Since I've always had a mind for business, I continued to take part in our business as often as possible. I listened intently to everything that my husband told me about the business.

I recall the day when he told me about meeting a young man named Joe Dudley. For years, Mr. Fuller had talked about wanting to meet a young person that he could trust to carry out his mission of helping others attain self-sufficiency. Meeting Joe Dudley got my husband all worked up and excited. He reminded me that after he had gone through more than 700,000 people, the right man for the job had finally come.

Mr. Fuller named Mr. Dudley president of Fuller Products, and made every attempt to clone himself in his protégé. When Fuller Products came upon hard times, it was Joe and Eunice Dudley who came to the rescue. Not only did they pour time and money into the business, but they also looked after Mr. Fuller personally. The Dudleys bought my husband a new car, hired many of our family members to work in their company, and even purchased the rights to the Fuller Products name to keep it in good standing.

Since my husband's death, Mr. Dudley has supported me, never failing to send me a check for $2,000 every month. Mr. Fuller was right when he foresaw that the right man, Mr. Dudley, had finally come along.

6

Overcome Adversity
With Determination

When I graduated from high school, going to college seemed the right thing to do. My parents always encouraged us to go to college, and all of my older brothers had obeyed their wishes. Since my parents could not afford to send all 11 of us to college, I planned to pay my own way through.

My oldest brother, Leroy, sent me money to go to Hartford, Connecticut. Later he got me a job in a chicken-processing plant to save money for school. I worked on a processing assembly line with many other people. As the line ran, my job was to pick the chickens from huge vats of ice and lay them out on the conveyor belt for processing.

I was a great worker. Whenever I got disgusted about my work, I just reminded myself how much I needed the job. If I was going to save money to go to college, I had to stay focused and determined. Some of my co-workers joked around and did not take their jobs seriously. But I was eager to give an honest day's work. I was making more money than I would have made doing farm work in the South. I was just happy to have a job, and I wanted my gratitude to show in both my attitude and the work I did. I thank my brother Leroy for helping to instill this attitude in me. He gave me copies of Dr. Norman Vincent Peale's Classic Books *The Power of Positive Thinking,* and

Enthusiasm Makes the Difference. Both have had profound effects on my life.

The books had a profound effect on his life as well. He later came to work with me and helped me to build one of the largest Fuller Products distributorships. In fact, he was one of the best Fuller Products salespeople, and sold part-time for many years while working as a director in New York City's Department of Social Services.

By December, I had saved enough money to pay my tuition for two quarters. I enrolled at North Carolina A & T State University, selecting poultry science as my major. To cover the expense of books and a place to live, I got a job working on the school's farm. Every morning, I fed the chickens and collected eggs. On weekends, I did housework for a professor on campus.

Nearly every day, I thought about how my father would encourage us to give our best to any job. Over the years, I've noticed that when I work hard and give an honest day's work, people around me try to do the same. Productivity breeds more productivity. I've also witnessed the way one bad seed in the group can cause the whole bunch to go bad. Negative thinkers and unhappy people can spread their bad spirit like a virus throughout a company.

When unproductive, uncaring people enter the business scene, otherwise hardworking people can be sent straight to the poorhouse. I've never wanted to be responsible for that kind of disaster, so regardless of the job I did, I tried to do it gratefully.

Fuller Products Company, the First Encounter

During the summer of 1957, I went to Brooklyn, New York, in search of full-time work. I needed a good-paying job to save money for my tuition. I moved into the basement of my aunt's home. In lieu of paying rent, I cleaned house for her. One day, I saw a young man about my age going door to door in the neighborhood. He was dressed in a business suit and appeared to be selling something from the black bag he was carrying. Being curious, I asked him what he was doing. He told me he was a dealer for Rose Meta Products.

The company was started by Rose Morgan, the wife of boxer Joe Louis, but eventually was purchased by a man named S. B. Fuller. The salesman also told me that working for Fuller Products was like being in business for himself.

"I can work when I want and make as much money as I want," he said. When I told him that I was looking for a job like his, he suggested that I come to the local office and buy a sales kit.

The next day, I went to Fuller Products branch in Brooklyn to learn more about the company. I discovered that Fuller Products was the largest black-owned company in the country. It had $10 million in annual revenue and more than 5,000 direct-sales representatives. The sales people at the office all told me they made a pretty good living selling Fuller Products. I was intrigued and eager to get started. I didn't know how well I would do as a salesman, but I certainly liked the idea of being able to determine the size of my paychecks. I paid $10 for a sales kit and joined the company.

My first day of work proved to me that being my own boss was not as fascinating as I had envisioned. My arms and legs ached with pain from walking all day. Even worse was the fact that I sold only $2.60 worth of products. When I got home that evening, I was exhausted. But before going to bed, I prayed. I didn't grumble about how bad my day had been. Instead, I thanked God for my job and for the money I had earned. I asked Him to help me become a successful dealer.

My prayer was answered. I started believing that I could sell and that people would buy from me. My sales steadily increased each week, and by the end of the summer, I was earning almost $100 a week in straight-commission sales. I saved enough money to pay my college tuition for a full year. My self-esteem soared, and I felt confident about my success as a salesman.

Realizing that I had the potential to earn a living for myself gave me a renewed sense of responsibility. I knew that from that summer on, I would never again have to look back and ask my parents for anything.

When I returned to North Carolina A & T in the fall, I brought my black bag of Fuller Products along with me. I continued to sell products during the school year. I enjoyed my job so much that I changed my major to business administration. During the school year, I came to appreciate the ability to work a flexible schedule. I also liked the fact that selling allowed me to meet interesting people. It served as an icebreaker of sorts. I followed the strategies I had learned in Brooklyn from Mr. John E. Johnson and others. I was attentive to my customer's needs and sensitive to their feelings. I wanted them to be satisfied with my service.

Care About Your Customers

Mr. Fuller, who genuinely cared about the welfare of others, encouraged every sales person at Fuller Products to adopt the same care and concern for customers. He emphasized to us that to be successful as salespeople, we had to take an interest in the personal development of our customers. We should entrust and empower our customers by sharing with them the philosophies of our company. Mr. Fuller wanted his sales force to do more than sell lotions, perfumes, and bubble bath on the streets. We had the dual responsibility of selling the importance of being job makers instead of job takers.

Before I would go on any sales call, I would review my products carefully. As I spoke with new customers, I listened attentively to their expectations of our products. I also rehearsed responses to those potential customers who would give me their ready-made excuses for not wanting to buy anything. I learned not to be discouraged by customers who would close the door in my face. "Have a nice day," I'd say through the crack of closing doors. I even practiced smiling. There is a saying that a smile cannot be bought, begged, borrowed, or stolen. In fact, it is of no earthly good to anybody until it is given away. It didn't take me long to realize that the more I smiled, the more my customers smiled. When I greeted them with a smile, they warmed up to me a lot faster, and our conversation was more friendly. So, I smiled a lot.

Learn From Successful People

For the next four summers, I returned to the Fuller Products branch in Brooklyn. I was hopeful each summer that I would earn even more money that I had the previous summer. I also hoped to learn more of Mr. Fuller's philosophies on selling and living. Having pioneered door-to-door selling in the black community, Mr. Fuller inspired a level of enthusiasm in his salespeople that made them the most energetic and determined group of people I'd ever been around.

Like my father, Mr. Fuller taught the importance of taking the initiative and being self-sufficient. He swore by a strong work ethic, and constantly quoted the Bible. He always emphasized that every man should earn his keep by the sweat of his own brow.

Mr. Fuller taught us that we could solve anything by simply going to work. "No matter what the situation, go to work," he would say. He believed that through hard work we could overcome any challenge and accomplish any goal.

Fuller Products became my mental gymnasium. Learning the *Fuller Way to Success* challenged my mind and exercised my brain. I was constantly required to think on my feet. Being a dealer demanded a lot of my attention. It gave me an understanding about the dedication and commitment it takes to become wealthy, successful, and personally fulfilled. My summer work played an important part in shaping my outlook on business in general.

Choose Your Life Partner Wisely

My summers in Brooklyn paid off in more than one way. The summer of 1960 was especially successful for me for reasons somewhat unrelated to work. It was while working out of the Brooklyn office that I met a woman who would play a major role in my future success and happiness. She would become my confidante, business partner, and wife. I first noticed her in a sales meeting.

Several of the top dealers at the company held regular competitions to see who could outsell the others. On this day, my strongest competitor, William Coston, had finally beaten me in sales. As a result of losing, I had to sit underneath a table for the whole meeting. There in the audience sat a beautiful young newcomer with long, black, thick hair and a pretty smile. After the meeting, she introduced herself as Eunice Mosley. Like most of the dealers during the summer months, Eunice had come to Brooklyn to earn money for college. She was a student at Talladega College in Talladega, Alabama.

Eunice's aunt was familiar with Fuller Products and suggested that Eunice call John E. Johnson, the branch manager, to inquire about a job. At the request of Mr. Johnson, she attended a sales meeting to learn more. Eunice was 17 years old and, by all accounts, she was all business. I noticed how organized and prepared she seemed to be, and I admired those traits.

I finally got around to asking Eunice on a date so that we could spend some time getting to know each other better. But when she discovered how old I was she said, "Boy, my mama would have a fit if she knew I even thought about dating an old man like you."

I hadn't considered our age difference an issue at all.

"What's six years?" I asked, laughing at her comment. What neither Eunice nor her mother knew was that my mind was made up: She was going to be my life partner. I wasn't going to take no for an answer.

Romance Without Finance Is a Nuisance

In Eunice, I found someone easy to open up to and talk with. I felt comfortable being around her. I learned that she was also staying with an aunt while in New York, and that we shared a lot of the same goals and dreams about the future.

We both wanted the most out of life. Eunice was determined and independent for her age. We even shared many of the same philosophies about life, and I enjoyed discovering how much we had in common.

As the summer progressed, Eunice made me promise that our romance would not interfere with work. She emphasized that our relationship had to be based on business before pleasure. At first, it was easy for me to stick to our plan. However, love is a strange thing.

The more time I spent with Eunice, the more of her time I wanted. I enjoyed her company and felt comfortable whenever we were together. But Eunice was tough. One of her favorite sayings was, "Romance without finance is a nuisance." She borrowed that phrase from Mr. John E. Johnson.

Eunice understood the power and importance of money. She knew that a lot could be accomplished when a person wasn't limited by lack of money. She lived by that philosophy. If she made $75.50, she'd save $75.00 and allow herself only the 50 cents to spend. She'd walk to work instead of paying for bus fare, and she'd go home to eat instead of spending money at restaurants.

She encouraged me to exceed my weekly sales quota, and after I agreed, she told me that if I didn't get my quota each week, then we couldn't date on that weekend. Well, as you can guess, I got very motivated to sell those products. In fact, it wasn't long before I was exceeding even the goals we set. One of my main goals was to marry Eunice, and in 1961 we were married and started our joint growth adventure together.

Growing and Learning to Operate a Business

For a while everything seemed to be progressing just as I had hoped. I was promoted to crew manager, and my sales were good. I was confident that my dream of being the next branch manager was well within reach. I encouraged Eunice to give up selling and take a job working in the office.

I wanted her to learn how the branch was run from the inside. A few couples in Fuller Products were beginning to buy their own distributorships, and I wanted Eunice and me to be prepared for the day we owned a shop of our own as well. My wife learned about the day-to-day operations of the company, while I focused on selling.

Eunice and I were very happy to be part of a successful black-owned company that was making such a difference in the world. We were loyal to Mr. Fuller, a rare visionary and entrepreneur. Our primary objective was to help carry out his vision of economic empowerment for blacks.

After we had saved a good amount of money and settled into our jobs with the company, Eunice and I decided to start a family. It wasn't the first time that we had thought about having a baby, but somehow now the time seemed right. We moved out of my aunt's home and got an apartment of our own. Eunice reminded me that no amount of money was too much when it came to providing a decent home for our child.

"Having children is a luxury, Joe," she said, "not just something we can jump right into." We planned carefully and dutifully saved almost every dime.

Raising a Family

In 1963, our first child, Joe Jr., was born. My wife had screened so many day-care facilities that I was beginning to wonder whether she'd ever find one that she trusted to look after little Joe. Then she met Ms. Hattie Butts, an older woman who cared for a few children in her home. She and Eunice got along well. Aunt Hattie, as the children would call her, was a kind, gentle lady who regarded our son as her own.

My excitement about becoming a father was coupled with a renewed energy and determination to succeed. I was incredibly motivated by the responsibility of my role. After all, I had a new mouth to feed. Shortly after Joe Jr. was born, Mr. Johnson, the branch manager, sent me to Baltimore for five weeks. He wanted me to be a troubleshooter for the company. My responsibility was to report back to him on ways that the company could improve its operations.

When I recall how much planning Eunice and I put into getting ready for Joe Jr., it leads me to wonder why so many young people today are having children. There are an alarming number of teen-age pregnancies, and the majority are to single mothers. I am disheartened at how nonchalantly they justify having babies when they cannot even afford to sustain their own lives, let alone the fragile life of a newborn child. National statistics indicate that it takes almost $330,000 to raise a child from birth to 18 years of age. That's a lot of money!

Young people jeopardize their futures by starting families too soon. I encourage you to tell any young persons contemplating sex to get their priorities in order. Before starting a family, you should first be about the business of securing your own places in the world. You need an education, a decent job, and a supportive spouse. It makes things so much easier.

I know that just thinking about how to raise our son left me feeling overwhelmed. There was so much that I wanted for him, so many characteristics I hoped he would develop. Even with all the time that work required, I had to save enough energy to spend time with my son. He and I spent many hours reading the Bible, just as my father had done with me. Once he learned to talk, we would discuss all sorts of things. I did my best to teach him humility, self-confidence, and a strong work ethic.

My teaching and time spent with my son reaped a tremendous reward. Joe Jr. received his undergraduate and MBA degrees from Northwestern University. He is currently our vice president of finance and has made major contributions in our marketing department.

In 1966 our second child—our oldest daugher, Ursula—was born. This new blessing from God further fanned my desire to become successful and be a good father and provider for my family.

Both Eunice and I spent more time discussing and developing goals and objectives that would permit us to learn more, earn more, and be in a postition to help the company grow. We now had two children to feed, educate, clothe, and nurture. We were determined to work as hard as possible to provide for all our family needs.

I was at that time a Fuller crew manager, but I set my heart and sights upon becoming the next Brooklyn branch-office manager.

The birth of Ursula and my desire to grow within Fuller Products worked together to help develop my deep belief in everyone's saving as much money as possible.

Shortly after Ursula's birth, I was talking with Mr. John Johnson about how I could develop and become a candidate for the next Brooklyn branch managership. During the conversation, I happened to mention that Sam Battle, one of the Fuller sales representatives, had saved $200 the previous week. I admitted that I had saved only $100 that week. My excuse was that with an additional child, I could not save any more. Mr. Johnson responded that not only could I save more, but also, now with Ursula, I had to save more.

As a result of Mr. Johnson's awakening remarks, I intensified my savings habits. I tell all our employees, customers, and associates that the savings habit—the habit of paying yourself first—is the key to any and all financial success. I owe Ursula a debt of gratitude for helping me recognize this myself.

Ursula earned both her undergraduate and law degrees at Harvard University. She is currently the corporate counsel for our company and head of the Dudley Cosmetics Division.

In 1973, six years after we had located in Greensboro, North Carolina, our business success was coupled with personal joy when Genea, our youngest daughter, was born. Eunice was so swamped with work during pregnancy that she almost didn't make it to the hospital in time. It was a miracle that Genea's birth didn't occur right at the office. When the labor pains began, my wife's secretary took notice. When she couldn't get Eunice to stop working and go to the hospital with any degree of expediency, she called the doctor herself. She then got Eunice on the phone and the doctor told her to come to the hospital at once.

Because we were so swamped with orders and audits that day, my wife was concerned about leaving with everything in limbo. As she struggled to give final instructions to the staff on the work that remained to be done, the doctor phoned again. "Mrs. Dudley, you've got to come here right now," he warned, "or else we're sending an ambulance over to your office." With that, my wife stopped work for the day and got a ride to the hospital. Genea was delivered within minutes of Eunice's arrival at the hospital.

Eunice and I built a new home to celebrate the birth of our daughter. We realized that with the birth of each of our children we had managed to move into nicer homes, although it wasn't necessarily planned that way. We were all the more grateful because of our decision always to put business first. Our new home was a mansion by some standards. It had more than 12 rooms, and we began to receive recognition from a variety of media sources. Unaccustomed to so much attention, we felt like celebrities. We used the media to impress on other people that it is possible for anyone to achieve the degree of success that we were enjoying.

When my wife returned to work, she was happy to learn that the office was functioning well and our sales were still rapidly increasing. This trend continued for the next two years. It all happened so fast that to many people it seemed as though we went from rags to riches overnight. Our salespeople were building new homes and buying Cadillacs and even investing money back into the company. I knew that we were being blessed. For so many years, everybody had listened to preaching about a day when we would have no financial worries.

I had talked until I was blue in the face about the day when we would have salespeople all over the country, and each one would be earning more than $25,000 a year. We had far surpassed that goal. We were celebrating and singing our new fight song: *"I wanna be rich— RICH, RICH. I'm gonna be rich—RICH, RICH!"*

Overcoming Frustration and Doubt

During the latter part of our stay in New York, my desire to be the next branch manager for the Brooklyn office was put on hold. Instead of being promoted to that position, I was made team captain. To make matters worse, I had to share the spotlight with my chief competitor in sales, Mr. William Coston.

I wasn't happy about the decision, and couldn't understand why we were both promoted to the same position. I felt that I had worked hard—much too hard, in fact, to share the lead with someone else. Each day I made my rounds door to door, hoping to prove my loyalty to the company. I had been a good team player and had demonstrated my leadership ability by recruiting and assisting newcomers into the company.

I had worked very hard to pattern myself after Mr. Fuller, but all of that seemed to be ignored. Even though I considered myself more experienced and better skilled to handle the job than Coston was, no one else acknowledged it. Finally, I came to the conclusion that Fuller Products Company just didn't appreciate me.

Angry and bitter, I decided to prove that it had made a mistake. I planned to go out and sell the socks off Coston. I would show everyone in Brooklyn, and at the home office in Chicago, that I was the best dealer ever. But somehow, my plan failed. Coston must have had the same idea, because out of nowhere, his sales soared higher and higher.

The number of new recruits he brought into the company also increased. And regardless of the number of hours I put into preparing speeches for our daily sales meetings, Coston had something that I didn't. He was an articulate and powerful speaker. I could pick wonderful topics to talk about, but because of my speech impediment, my presentation left something to be desired. I could not speak with the same style and eloquence that William Coston could.

Completely outdone, I became more and more frustrated as Coston gained more and more attention. The more success he enjoyed, the more depressed I became. It wasn't long before I was going to the doctor every other week because of problems with my nerves. Dr. Green, our family doctor, prescribed some pills to help me relax. I admit that I probably needed them, but taking those pills made me feel a little too relaxed. I didn't feel on top of what was going on.

I was moving in slow motion at a time when I wanted more energy than ever before. I stopped taking the medicine and tried to cope with my stress, but it was harder than I realized. Despite my best intentions to move the mountain in front of me, worry and frustration set in. My sales started to drop and my enthusiasm declined.

My attitude eventually took a toll on my family life as well. Eunice was growing more impatient about my declining sales each week. We still had a family to support, and what was more upsetting was the fact that there was nothing anybody could do to pull me out of my slump. It was obvious that I was causing the stress on my own.

Don't Throw in the Towel too Early

With my health, job, and my family at risk, I decided to throw in the towel. I didn't need a job that caused me so much turmoil. I decided to take my family home to North Carolina and start a hog farm. Long before I learned about Fuller Products, my dream had been to raise hogs. I figured out that I could develop a pretty progressive hog operation and do well for myself. I didn't need to continue selling Fuller products for the rest of my life, and I sure didn't want to work for a company that I didn't think appreciated my hard work.

When Mr. Fuller heard about my resignation, he asked me to come to Chicago. He wanted me to focus on recruiting new dealers into the company. I suspected that he would try to persuade me to stay with the company, but I had made up my mind that nothing he could say would make me change my plans.

"Help Me Raise People"

The Chicago office had sales meetings each morning. During the first meeting I attended, Mr. Fuller told everybody about my decision to leave the company. He had a knack for addressing dealers' personal situations in the sales meetings. I had seen him do it with other dealers before.

Often, he would devote entire meetings to issues relating to one person. I had witnessed both men and women breaking down under the pressure of being the center of attention. I'd seen just as many come to different conclusions or change their minds about whatever situation they were facing.

Visitors to our meetings might think Mr. Fuller was being cruel, but we all knew that he spoke out of love. Everybody listened attentively as he made sense of our dilemmas. I had to admit that it was a pretty slick tactic, but I refused to be taken in by it. For the next month, Mr. Fuller hammered on me during the sales meetings. He talked about my plan to return to North Carolina and raise hogs.

One day he called on me, saying, "Mr. Dudley, why don't you tell the group about the kind of life you envision as a farmer, and how much money you'll be earning?"

I was reluctant to speak, but I refused to appear shaken by his question. I attempted to put into words all the thoughts and plans that had preoccupied my mind for the past few months. As I spoke, I saw some obvious holes in my plan—things I had not considered; questions I hadn't asked. My words slowed when I realized that the image I projected didn't sound nearly as rewarding as my career with Fuller Products. I began to have doubts about whether I could give my wife the same quality of life if I was a hog farmer. I stopped talking and sat there speechless. Mr. Fuller moved on to another subject.

After the meeting, Mr. Fuller approached me with a look of sympathy. He said, "Mr. Dudley, you're much too talented to just give up on your career with the company." He challenged me to stick with the business. Then he offered me an alternative to my frustrating postition in New York.

"If you want to get out of the Brooklyn Branch, then let me suggest an alternative," he said. He told me that for a $2,000 investment, Eunice and I could be independent distributors for the company. He said there were only a few distributorship opportunities available, but if we were interested, he would help us get started. My aunt, who had invested a lot of money in Fuller Products, agreed to give up some of her return investment to help Eunice and me pay for the distributorship. Mr. Fuller was open to this arrangement, if we agreed.

Later that day, I spent considerable time thinking of our own distributorship and whether we could do it. In thinking it over, it occurred to me that Eunice and I had been given the best possible preparation for this opportunity.

Mr. Samuel Dicks, a long-time Fuller Branch manager in Brooklyn and Atlanta, had spent many hours with Eunice and me teaching us how to sell, to recruit, and to manage a Fuller branch effectively. We were very fortunate to learn from Mr. Dicks, who was a cornerstone of Fuller Products' success. Mr. Dicks took a personal interest in our direct-sales training and development. Because of this, I felt comfortable, considering Mr. Fuller's offer.

In addition to Mr. Dicks, the following successful Fuller branch managers were also strong influences on our future success:

Leroy Cooper of Chicago; Henry and Tina Tarver of New Jersey and New York; Lucious Woods of Philadelphia, Pennsylvania; Frank Smalls of New York City; Joe Knight of East Orange, New Jersey; Charlie Stevenson of Brooklyn, New York; Archie Gregg of Baltimore, Maryland; James Mahone of Cleveland, Ohio; Charles McSwain of Newark, New Jersey; Harold Nash of Baltimore; Bernard and Ann Lacewell of Baltimore; John Lawson of Dallas, Texas; Earline Scroggins of Brooklyn; Keys O'Kelly of Birmingham, Alabama; Idonia Anderson of Memphis, Tennessee; Louise Carlos of Hartford, Connecticut; and Charlie Steed of East Orange.

These individuals were all significant contributors to Fuller Products' success and provided tremendous preparation and support to us as we developed our own Fuller distributorship and, eventually, Dudley Products, Inc. Eunice and I are eternally grateful to every one of them.

That night, I called Eunice to tell her about Mr. Fuller's offer. We talked about opening our own branch in Brooklyn. I agreed to discuss it with Mr. Fuller the next morning. Eunice told me not to get my hopes up about having our branch in Brooklyn. She reminded me that even though Brooklyn was a large borough of New York City, the branch already there wouldn't welcome competition. Eunice was right. A few days later, Mr. Fuller told me that some people were apprehensive about our request. He said that to keep everybody happy, he wanted us to consider opening our branch someplace else.

Mr. Fuller didn't want me to feel discouraged about the situation. I'm sure he sensed my frustration, and probably suspected that my original intent to be a hog farmer would resurface. As I turned to walk away, he put his hand on my shoulder and said, "Mr. Dudley, instead of raising hogs, you belong here helping me to raise people." He assured me that there was plenty of opportunity within the company for my wife and me if only we would consider another territory.

Later that evening, I sat alone in my hotel room and rethought our conversation. He believed that I could help him raise people. From my earliest contact with Fuller Products, I understood and agreed with the organization's mission. I had stayed with the company for almost ten years because I believed in that mission. I wanted to see people, especially black people, empowered and self-sufficient. I wanted to play a part in making that happen.

My father had reared me by those principles. The thought that I might be able to share that wisdom with others, lead the way, and help create jobs was exciting.

"I can do it!" I thought. But if I was to raise people, I had to set an example. I couldn't quit when the chips were down. I had to believe in the mission 100% or not at all. I challenged myself to do just that.

I sensed, for the first time, that I had a purpose in life. I was destined to help raise people! I credit Mr. Fuller with helping me to realize my mission in life. I followed him without hesitation, question, or reservation, hoping to learn more about raising people.

Developing Our Fuller Distributorship

When Mr. Fuller subsequently suggested that Eunice and I open our new distributorship in Alabama, we decided that I would go first to set up our business and find us a home. Later, she and the children could join me there. With my bags packed, I left Brooklyn. I planned to stop over in Greensboro for a brief visit with some close friends who were business people in their own right. They discouraged me from going to Alabama. They talked about all of the prejudice and racial injustice there. Even though most of the South was up in arms over the battle for civil rights, Alabama, they said, was the central headquarters. The last thing I wanted to do was take the hard road. I was hoping to make a fresh start. I wanted an easier way. I needed a good territory where I could grow and prosper without too many conflicts. I needed allies, not enemies.

I got up the nerve to call Mr. Fuller. I told him that I didn't want to move to Alabama. Mr. Fuller was understanding. He asked me to consider Tennessee, but I didn't want to move there either. I told Mr. Fuller that I preferred staying in North Carolina, where I had a support system. I had family and good friends in the business community who could counsel and direct me as I worked to make my distributorship the best in the company. With Mr. Fuller's approval, I called Eunice and told her about the change of plans.

I am forever indebted to my brother William, who is a very successful veterinarian in Minneapolis, Minnesota, for the advice and assistance he gave me in getting started in this business. William also loaned me money to get the Greensboro Fuller branch started, and also loaned me the money to buy our first home. Without his assistance, we would have been unable to make this move so easily.

I was so excited about opening our new branch that I quickly found some office space and a home for my family. Eunice and the children then joined me in Greensboro. For a while, things were going well. I hired a few salespeople to work for us and assumed my new role as a manager. I prepared speeches for our daily sales meetings and worked hard to motivate our dealers to go out and sell, sell, sell!

I was content with being a manager; so content that I stopped going on my daily sales route. After meetings each day, I would work in the office for a while, and then take the rest of the afternoon off. Being a manager required thinking, I believed, and I couldn't afford to focus my energy on both leading and selling at the same time.

Although we were making less money than we could have with my selling, I figured that it was just a matter of time before our salespeople would get the hang of things and our distributorship would be making a profit. Until then, we'd just have to make do on a lot less money.

"I Can Do Bad All By Myself"

One day, I came home early from work to find all my clothes in a pile just inside the front door. I barged through the house yelling to Eunice for an explanation. Startled by my loud entrance, she grabbed a hammer and waved it in my face. "Shut up and listen," Eunice hollered at me. "Joe, I can do bad all by myself. I don't need you around here making matters worse. I've put up with your laziness for as long as I can stand it. But I can't take it anymore! You've got to get off your high horse about this management thing and get to work selling products. We can't continue to live like this. Bills are still coming in, and nobody cares that we don't have the money to pay them." With that, she slammed the hammer down on a table, turned and walked away.

For a moment, I stood there in the middle of the room, shocked and confused. What just happened here? Realizing that this was no time for conversation, I opened the door, stepped over my clothes and left. For almost an hour, I walked, until eventually I wound up back at the office. As I sat there in the dark, I asked myself whether I was really being lazy. Was I really justified in not selling products?

Leaders Are Supposed to Lead By Example

I knew then that I had been wrong. Leaders are supposed to lead by example, but that's not what I had been doing. How could I expect my dealers to make great sales when they witnessed me doing so much talking about motivation and then going home for the afternoon. I had to change. If I wanted to keep my family together, then for sure I had to change.

Desperate to make up with Eunice, I picked up the phone and called home. She was about to hang up when she heard my voice, but I begged her to hear me out.

"If you will give me six weeks—just six weeks—then I promise to do better," I said. "I love you and I love our children. Please give me another chance," I pleaded.

Eunice had sympathy for me. We made up, and I went back home. Beginning the very next morning, I went to work. I gave my sales meeting, and then hit the streets selling products. Over the next six weeks, I worked around the clock to get the distributorship on its feet. Eunice got a job working for a law firm that happened to be in the same building as our office. Each morning she would take the children to school and then open the office for our meetings. During her lunch break, she would return to the office to distribute merchandise to the dealers. After work, my wife would collect money from the dealers and do bookkeeping.

Just Go to Work

"To overcome any challenge, just go to work," I recalled Mr. Fuller saying. And that's what I did. I gained more customers, and my sales increased. My spirit and enthusiasm came back. Facing the loss of my family forced me to get my priorities in order. It's unfortunate that it took such an ugly situation to make me consider what is most important. But as with many people, my ego had gotten in the way of my ability to think straight. I couldn't see the signs right in front of me.

Every once in a while we all need to take time to re-evaluate where we're headed in life. If it's only for a few minutes a day, the impact will be monumental. Not too many people devote time to thinking about their purpose in life. They just coast along, taking life as it comes. That's what I had done. But if you are motivated to make a difference in the world, then you will regularly take a few minutes to think about where you are headed. How grateful for life can you be if all you do is get up in the morning, go to work, come home, eat dinner, watch television, and then go to bed? What purpose are you serving? What goals are you achieving?

A man once approached me who was troubled about his failed relationship with the woman he loved. She had left him for someone else. He blamed her for every bad experience he had faced since their break-up. He claimed that it was all her fault. After he explained each of his dilemmas, I said, "It's not her fault, it's *yours.*"

His mouth dropped open. He hadn't considered the role he'd played in any of his misfortune. I said, "You should not have put her in a position in which she would consider leaving you. You forced her to leave by not doing what you should have been doing to keep her. If I were you, I would go to that woman and thank her for showing you how weak you really are."

He looked at me strangely, and then walked away. Obviously, I had not said what he wanted to hear, but I did tell him the truth. I'd been down that road.

Put Business Before Pleasure

My life was again consumed by work. As our distributorship grew and started to make a nice profit, Eunice left her job with the law firm and came back to the business to help me. We poured all of our energy into the company. Growing meant working long hours, and we often missed family reunions, weddings, parties, and other special occasions for our families. Business before pleasure, we reasoned. We believed that the day would come when everyone could look at our business accomplishments and understand why it had been so important for us to stay focused on work. We knew that down the road our families would forgive our absences.

Our branch became the top-producing distributorship of Fuller Products, beating even the branch in Brooklyn. I was happy. I continued to do all the things that Mr. Fuller had taught me. I ran our office exactly as he ran the corporate office in Chicago. Everything Mr. Fuller advised, I did. I was a follower and a believer. Nothing he ever said was taken lightly. I just went to work implementing all of his strategies for success. We stayed in touch often, and on several occasions, he visited me in Greensboro.

We were blessed at that time to have my younger brothers, MacArthur and George Washington, working with us on the sales team while they both attended A & T State University. I personally re-cruited both of them. After completing veterinary medicine school, MacArthur assisted me financially on several occasions. After developing an allergy to cats and dogs, Mac returned. He is currently working for the company. He and George Washington are both sales managers.

Growing Pains

I worked with our salespeople to help expand our territory. I helped our best recruiters to get cars so that they could attract good people into the company. I was spending a lot of money and, since I didn't want my wife to know about the debt I was creating, I hid the receipts in a suitcase. When Charles Knight and Paul Gilmer, two of our best people, needed cars, I put up the money to help them. At the same time, Eunice and the children were relying on public transportation to get around. I believed that if we sacrificed a little in the beginning, the results down the road would be monumental.

One day, as Eunice was packing for a trip, she discovered my hidden receipts. She wasn't as upset about the money I'd spent as she was about the fact that I'd tried to hide it from her. I promised not to keep any more secrets and to include her in everything from then on. I also bought my wife a car. It wasn't a great car, but it sure beat riding the bus.

The Fuller Products Crisis

As our distributorship grew, I knew that Fuller Products was having financial trouble. The company was facing bankruptcy as a result of a national boycott started by a number of civil-rights leaders who misinterpreted its self-reliance philosophy. Mr. Fuller believed that blacks should work and do business together, buying their own enterprises instead of campaigning for the right to patronize businesses where they were not welcome.

Eunice and I were concerned about the company's situation, and eager to help. We invested a lot of our personal savings, and even asked our family and friends to invest. We couldn't stand the thought of Fuller Products, a company we cherished so much, going out of business.

Although we remained dedicated and hopeful that all of the challenges facing the company would eventually run their course, the impact was beginning to put a strain on our ability to do business from the Greensboro branch. It became increasingly difficult to get our orders for products filled. The home office couldn't afford to pay vendors for all the ingredients they needed to manufacture our product line. So each month, our inventory dwindled.

Eventually, we were unable to get enough from Fuller Products to service even minimal needs. We had to find our own products to meet the needs of our customers and for our sales force to survive to keep the Fuller philosophy alive.

"What If We Made Our Own Products?"

My wife and I spent many hours talking about our dilemma. We knew there had to be a way out. God wouldn't close one door without opening another, we believed. We'd come too far by faith to lose everything now. Just as I felt myself becoming more and more consumed with stress over the situation, I got an idea. I went to Eunice and asked her: "What if we made our own products?"

I suggested that if we developed our own products, the dealers could continue working, and we could keep enough inventory to fill orders. We hoped that by selling a new product we could maintain our business until Fuller Products could get back on its feet. We both agreed that it was at least worth a try.

I went to the public library to find out how we could get started. In the process, I learned about a man in Richmond, Virginia, who had developed his own product line. His company was called Rosebud

Beauty Products, and his top-selling product was Rosebud Hair Pomade.

Eunice and I scheduled a meeting with him, and we were surprised to learn that he was working from his garage. But he was making good money. He showed us how he made the products, and gave us some useful information on how we could get started.

When he told us that he was interested in finding a buyer for his small business, we eagerly negotiated an agreement to buy it. I got busy researching his formula to make sure it was a good-quality product. With the rights to his company, we renamed the product Dudley's Scalp Special. I was in the kitchen making Scalp Special every night. As I completed a batch, my wife would test it to make sure it came out right. Then she would package it. It was the same routine every night. I would mix the ingredients and Eunice would test and then package the product in old containers that we obtained from local beauty salons. We would wash and sanitize the containers, then fill them up with our Scalp Special.

When we ran out of containers, we'd use old jelly or mayonnaise jars—whatever we could find around the house. My wife would type the labels and help Joe Jr. and Ursula glue each label on. Everybody had a part to play. We were building a family business.

Our sales people were excited about the new product, and our customers readily accepted it. I tried to keep everybody motivated, while assuring them that our goal was to keep everybody happy and working until things looked brighter for Fuller Products.

Finding the Greater Advantage

Just as we got back on our feet, another challenge presented itself. The city licensing department served us with a "cease and desist" notice. It argued that our business was more retail-oriented than professional, so we were in violation of a zoning ordinance.

Prior to this, we had begun to suspect that something wasn't on the up-and-up. Someone informed me that the building owner couldn't handle the fact that we were a successful, minority-owned company. These allegations made sense of the petty complaints we had been getting from him. It seemed obvious to us that he was using every tactic he could think of to get us out.

We were evicted from the building, but as it turned out we didn't have to move very far. There was empty retail space directly across the street in a strip mall. After obtaining a retail license, we moved into the store. We named it "Dudley's Beauty Center and Salon," and stocked the shelves with our products and those from other manufacturers.

As the afro and wig era emerged, we sold a variety of wigs, hair pieces, and beauty aids. Mrs. Dudley ran the store and continued to do bookkeeping for our dealers. In the back of the store, we continued to hold daily sales meetings and demonstrations. The success of our first store led us to open new stores throughout North Carolina, South Carolina, Georgia, Virginia, and New York.

My sister Mardecia, whom I named "Baby Ruth" when she was a baby, worked with us on weekends at the time we were making products in the kitchen. Ruth was teaching in Danville, Virginia, during the week. She also loaned us money to help finance our growth and development. She was an early vice president in the Dudley Products Company, and is still a stockholder in our company. Her daughter Vernita has worked with the company during summer months.

We were doing well. Our products were a success, and we were making a very good profit on our retail sales. Just months before, we had considered it an obstacle that we couldn't get our hands on enough Fuller Products. But as soon as we jumped that hurdle, greater opportunities poured in. It was amazing to me that one small challenge could turn itself into the greatest opportunity for growth we'd ever experienced—proof again that *for every disadvantage there is an equal or greater advantage.*

If you've been faced with obstacles and challenges, then you can appreciate the fact that there is a benefit or a positive aspect to every negative experience. Although you may not see it at first, it's there. Stay focused on the bright side, and with faith, you'll jump hurdles and climb mountains faster than the swiftest animal. Likewise, be on the lookout for potential crises. The minute you detect a challenge coming your way, take action. Create a sense of urgency.

Dudley Salon Exclusives

I made friends with several cosmetologists in our area as a result of visiting them to obtain empty containers for our products. As I became more acquainted with those professionals, several shared their ideas on how we could better service their businesses.

Many of the cosmetologists told me about their need for an exclusive line of products that would not be sold in retail stores. They explained that having a professional-only line would have great impact on revenues in their salons. Eager to assist, Eunice and I reached agreements with a number of major well-known manufacturers to sell their products to licensed cosmetologists in the Southeast region. It was agreed that these products would be available exclusively to professional cosmetologists and would not be available in stores.

I spent a considerable amount of time training our sales managers on ways to introduce the products to the salons. Our sales managers then started calling on salons, selling the products, and telling cosmetologists that these products would be sold only to them, and not in stores.

The Big Switch

For all of our training and hard work, what we got in return was a major disappointment. Later, people noticed that these same products were beginning to be found in more and more retail stores. This meant the manufacturers had not made them exclusive as agreed. They had violated the terms of our agreement. We, along with the cosmetologists, had been used to introduce the products, create interest, and pave the way for retail selling in the stores. We had done all of the marketing for them and had persuaded people to try these products. We essentially got them using the products, then the manufacturers pulled the rug out from under us.

In Partnership With Professional Cosmetologists

We responded to the dilemma by expanding the Dudley product line into a professional line. We would manufacture the products. We would control and distribute them to cosmetologists.

We told cosmetologists that they could switch over to our brand and get our 100% guarantee. In partnership with them, we would never, ever put the products in retail stores. At that time, only a handful of other companies were making such promises, and many of them had already begun to go back on their word. We won back the trust of many of the cosmetologists, and our products sold quickly.

Cosmetologists from all over the country began placing orders. People in places we'd never heard of were calling to find out where they could get Dudley products. We hired more salespeople and sent them to cities up and down the East Coast and across the Midwest to win over their cities with our new products.

Although Eunice and I were still hopeful that Fuller Products would one day re-emerge from its financial eclipse, we were forced by the demand for our own product to switch our primary focus to the up-and-coming Dudley Products Company.

Millionaire By 40

By 1975, Dudley Products had annual sales in excess of $1.5 million. Eunice and I reached a welcome new plateau: We were millionaires—self-made millionaires, to be precise. We were very grateful. We stressed to almost everyone we met that they could do it, too. All it takes is a little faith and a lot of hard work, we preached. We pleaded with our employees, friends, and others to get serious about their careers and get excited about all of the opportunity out there just waiting around for motivated, enthusiastic people to take advantage of it.

Fuller Crisis Continues

As we enjoyed the success of our company, Eunice and I were nonetheless saddened that Mr. Fuller was not having the same good fortune. We invested more money in the company and even purchased the Brooklyn branch, where Eunice and I first met. I felt some small satisfaction in making that purchase. Not only was I helping the company, but I was also achieving a sense of closure by buying the branch that once eluded me.

Don't Quit

WHEN things go wrong, as they sometimes will,
When the road you're trudging seems all uphill,
When the funds are low and the debts are high,
And you want to smile, but you have to sigh,
When care is pressing you down a bit—
Rest if you must, but don't you quit.

LIFE is queer with its twists and turns,
As everyone of us sometimes learns,
And many a failure turns about
When we might have won had we stuck it out.
Don't give up, though the pace seems slow—
You may succeed with another blow.

OFTEN the goal is nearer than
It seems to a faint and faltering man
Often the struggler has given up
When he might have captured the victor's cup;
And he learned too late when the night came down,
How close he was to the golden crown.

WALKING BY FAITH

SUCCESS is failure turned inside out—
The silver tint of the clouds of doubt,
And you never can tell how close you are;
It may be near when it seems afar
So stick to the fight when you're hardest hit—
It's when things seem worst that you mustn't quit.

—Edgar Guest

CHAPTER

7

Accept Challenges in Faith

Answering the Call

In the spring of 1976, I was surprised by a particular phone call that came from Mr. Fuller in Chicago. After exchanging pleasantries, Mr. Fuller told me that he was having a tough time turning the company around. He had been diagnosed with Parkinson's disease and as a result, his energy and strength were drained. He told me that he was too tired to continue the fight. He wasn't sure how much longer he could hold out by himself.

"With a new leader at the helm," Mr. Fuller said, "I think the company could be revitalized. It's going to take someone with enough initiative to seek out what's in the best interest of Fuller Products."

I sat thinking as Mr. Fuller continued to talk.

"Mr. Dudley, I need someone who understands my vision and believes in it," he said, "I need someone who will continue to fight to raise people."

"Who could possibly take the place of S. B. Fuller?" I pondered. I sat in silence on the other end of the telephone as my mentor, the greatest influence in my life, sat describing the kind of person it would take to replace him.

As he ended his statement, Mr. Fuller said something that took me completely by surprise. He asked me to step in as president of Fuller Products.

"Me?" I asked, hearing the quiver in my own voice.

"Yes, you Mr. Dudley," he said. "You can do it; I know you can."

I was astonished that he would even consider me. Sure, I had trained under him and even developed a deep admiration for him; but I couldn't be him. I could feel the sincerity in each word Mr. Fuller said. I knew it took a lot for him to make this phone call, but I wasn't sure. His were big shoes to fill, and I didn't know whether I could do it.

Mr. Fuller assured me that he would be by my side to help me until I got the hang of things.

"And Mr. Dudley," he said, "there's no mistaking the fact that you can run this company."

My anxiety was replaced with confidence. If Mr. Fuller is there to help me, then maybe I can do it, I thought. I certainly wanted to be able to help the man who had helped me. This might be my only chance to do so. Without another moment's hesitation, I said, "Yes, Mr. Fuller, I'll take over as president."

Upon hearing the news, many people, including my family, thought I had lost my mind.

"What will happen to Dudley Products?" they asked.

I really didn't have an answer. The next time I spoke with Mr. Fuller, I told him that he didn't have to worry about Dudley Products' interfering with my duties as president. I told him that I would be 100% about the business of revitalizing Fuller Products. But Mr. Fuller wouldn't hear of it. He suggested that I move Dudley Products' corporate headquarters to Chicago. That way, he said, I could run both companies.

With all the logistics decided, I sold most of our retail stores and turned over management of a few to our loyal employees. Most of our sales and office staff agreed to move to Chicago along with us. About 20 salespeople stayed behind. My wife and I allowed them to set up residence in the home we had built. A few months later, everybody said their good-byes and car-pooled to Chicago.

Hello Chicago, Hello Snow

At first, Eunice was excited about living in the big city, but she was about to change her mind and go home when the first snowstorm hit. She had never been fond of the snow, particularly when it came to traveling in it. Regardless of what was going on, if there was snow on the ground, Eunice reminded me that she would not be leaving the house "for any reason, for anybody."

Knowing what was in my best interest, I had no qualms about her decision. Mr. Fuller, however, was of a different mindset. He said, "Eunice, you are not a cream puff. A little bit of snow will not cause you to melt. As long as there are buses, cars, and subways getting around the streets of Chicago, I expect you to find a way to get into this office."

I can only guess that their confrontation was more than Mr. Fuller had bargained for, because just a few days later, he postponed our usual sales meeting so he could give the entire staff a lesson on how to drive in the snow. One thing is for sure: Nowadays, some people are startled to see my wife out buzzing through the streets of our small town when there's snow on the ground. But Eunice learned to get around in the snow and to master driving during a Chicago snowstorm, which represents a much bigger challenge than taking on a North Carolina snow.

Fear, Success, and Phobia

I faced a different sort of fear about the big city, and it was intensified a hundred times over when I learned that our apartment at that time was in Lake Point Tower, the world's tallest apartment building. Our new home was on the 53rd floor, and I'm afraid of heights. To make matters worse, Eunice had my desk positioned so that it faced the window. I couldn't believe it.

Although she had redecorated and made our home quite a showplace, I was also mindful of the fact that the only thing separating me from the ground 53 stories below was a simple glass pane. Eunice believed that the beautiful surroundings would help me overcome my fear of heights. I, on the other hand, was convinced that I would have a heart attack and die. Somehow I got settled into the space, and even managed to enjoy the view of the skyline once or twice.

Unfortunately, I was never totally comfortable so far up. To this day, I still get queasy over high altitudes. In fact, when we travel, it's not uncommon for a hotel to offer us their penthouse suite. "Not for me," I say, "I'd prefer a room on the first floor, please."

"The Big House"

We bought a house for members of our sales force who didn't have a place to live. It was also there for our new salespeople. We called it "The Big House." On any given day, 20 or more people would live in that house. We had only one key made, and we entrusted it to one salesperson. All of the sales people had to be out of the house in time to make the 9 a.m. sales meeting each day, and the doors of the house were not reopened until dusk. We left them no choice but to go out and work all day—just as we did.

During this time, we recruited many people from the Virgin Islands and elsewhere in the Caribbean. We also recruited salespeople from the West Coast. I conducted more than 40 demonstrations each day, and others followed suit. We were all serious about rebuilding Fuller Products.

Fire in My Bones

I again submitted to Mr. Fuller's leadership and sought to gain more wisdom from the man I most admired. Often, he would tell me to slow down and spend more time in the office learning from him. But I was on fire. I had made up my mind that I was going to take Chicago by storm. I imagined how much joy it would bring to him to

106

see his company back on top. I also imagined how grateful I would feel for the opportunity to play a part in making that happen and making improvements to the company.

With time, I learned to lead effectively and to manage the large corporation. Through trial and error, I also learned how to maintain a harmonious office environment and reduce conflicts. I learned more about the hair-care and beauty-aids industry than all my previous years of experience had allowed. I viewed the whole industry from a new perspective. Instead of seeing everything through the eyes of a salesman, I learned that there is a much bigger picture. I saw the importance of a good manufacturing crew and a strong office team and how, when all departments complement one another, work is so much more enjoyable.

When we didn't have enough products to keep our salespeople busy, I went to work negotiating with other companies so that we could market their items. We even sold Bibles once: on the street, door to door, enthusiastically getting people to buy the word of God.

From that experience, I came to understand that sales are not as dependent upon the product so much as they are upon the salesperson. People bought whatever we sold because they liked our personalities, they understood our mission and they wanted to play a part. That's something that I have never forgotten.

Mr. Fuller monitored my professional growth. Always being a very methodical and organized person, he encouraged me to run the office more efficiently.

"It just takes a little common sense," he'd say. I studied Mr. Fuller's method. He always kept a very structured schedule, so I began to plan my work days as well. I learned to manage my time and to document important matters in writing. As I settled into a daily routine, I felt more at ease about my responsibility.

Eunice's Role Expands

Eunice was also growing professionally. She was purchasing agent for the manufacturing plant, where she learned the practicalities of purchasing as well as the proper way to run a plant. It wasn't long before Eunice assumed responsibility for all aspects of manufacturing in our own company as well. Her knowledge and experience accounts for the success we have enjoyed in our present manufacturing plant. Our customers frequently comment on how efficient our manufacturing and distributions systems work.

Eunice and I had always tried to set a certain standard at work. We wanted others to see that we worked just as hard as we expected them to work. We were always on time and even willing to put in overtime to get the job done. Everybody was expected to follow suit; even our children came to work with us when school was out. Our employees were encouraged to bring their kids into the office as well.

"Let them learn the value of work early on," I'd say.

The children were given specific jobs to do, and they worked alongside their parents to help out. Being included in the work made the children closer to their parents. One of the things all of the kids loved about coming to work on weekends or holidays was getting to eat Brown's Chicken for lunch or dinner. Even my oldest daughter, Ursula, had fond memories of mealtimes at the office. We were all convinced that Brown's had the best Southern-fried chicken Chicago had to offer. We would sit and enjoy juicy, golden chicken like one big, happy family.

Troubles Mount

By 1983, I was losing enthusiasm. In spite of all the time, energy, and money I had invested in the company, our growth was slow in happening. Although Fuller Products was doing better after we moved to Chicago, the company was still struggling. There were few assets and hardly any available cash. I felt that we still had a long, long way to go in our work to turn the company around.

It had been seven years, I kept thinking to myself. The stress was lying heavily on me. My wife and I had spent most of our money. We couldn't afford to invest any more money in the company, since it was at the expense of our own company. Things became all the more difficult; then Mr. Fuller's health problems got worse. All the people seemed to have their own ideas about how the company should be run, and it was a big challenge just trying to keep everybody happy.

God Sent Me an Angel

Even during these troubling times, I resolved never to make excuses. I personally believe that instead of making excuses for difficult times, people should have faith and look within themselves for solutions. I also believe, as I have said, that in every disadvantage is a seed of an equivalent or greater advantage.

While our company was operating in Chicago, we found ourselves in typically cold, cold Chicago winters, with big bills and little money. My main problem was the really big building in which we operated. The building's windows, walls, and everything else were poorly insulated and provided little or no defense from Chicago's infamous wind. Obviously, the more the wind blew into our poorly insulated building, the higher our heating bills were. In fact, our gas bill averaged $18,000 per month at a time when we were doing little or no business.

We were forced to borrow money and do anything we could just to stay in business. Our daily routine focused at times on just two activities: trying to borrow money from everyone we met, and using anything we could to try to fill the holes in our windows and walls.

In spite of our difficulty in borrowing money, I was determined to find a way out of our situation. Since I am a strong believer in reading for inspiration and motivation, I started reading Robert Collier's book, *The Secret of the Ages.*

The author points out in this classic that in times of difficulty you have to exercise the trust of a swimmer. You *must* trust. His message goes like this: "You must compare the man who trusts his life to prayer with the swimmer who trusts himself to the water."

It was about three o'clock in the morning when I came across Collier's insight that if you know the truth, the sea will carry you. If you do certain things, you will swim quietly, calmy, serenely, happily. You won't mind if the water goes right over you. You won't become frustrated because you don't know what will happen; you will keep on going. At that point, I prayed and decided to *Walk By Faith.* I lived on the 53rd floor of Lake Point Tower and decided to walk down all 53 floors. As I walked down the steps, I prayed again. I walked to Lake Shore Drive and walked along the lake.

As I walked, I talked to God. I said "You told me what to do. I have followed Your instructions to the best of my ability. You said ask; You said seek; You said knock. Now, Lord, I've done all of those things. All I need is $50,000 to fix these windows; $50,000, that's all I need. The people across the street have their big building; you gave it to them. I'm your child also. I'm not asking for anyone else's building, I'm only asking for $50,000."

I then turned around and walked back to Lake Point Tower. I walked back up those 53 floors with a new feeling within me.

About two days later, I met a lady who said she had seen me a couple of times.

"Young man," she said, "you need some money, don't you?"

"Yes, I do," I told her. "Let me show you why I need money."

"Well, you don't have a lot of time," she observed after I had explained the situation. "So send two of your trusted people over to my house at lunch time."

I did, and when they returned, they brought back a $40,000 loan from this lady—my Angel.

While she was withdrawing the funds, the bankers asked her "What are you going to do with that money? Why are you taking that money out?"

She let them know it was none of their business. She just sent it and did not ask me to come and get it. She respected me and my position enough that she sent me $40,000. Later on, she came to my plant and became an employee. She worked as a plant worker for minimum wage. She even prayed over our products. She once said to me, "I'll be with you until you become very rich." I would sometimes walk around the plant, and she'd look at me and ask me to come over. She would pull out a blank check and say, "Write down what you need."

While the money she loaned me was very important, one of the greatest things was that she had trust in me, and that she would put her money into the business.

I continued to recruit a lot of people back then. Many of them were on drugs. There was this one young lady—a drug addict—that we put to work in our plant. Mrs. Olivia Jackson (My Angel), helped me to save this one. I would work on her for a while, and she would work on her for a while, until we convinced her that she should do better.

We would send some of the recruits to school and anywhere else to get them off drugs. Mrs. Jackson worked in the plant and really enjoyed helping the people who worked there. Throughout this particular time, we continued periodically to need money. But we still kept on. Every time we needed something, Mrs. Jackson helped. Eventually, she wound up lending us more than $100,000.

When I got ready to move from the building in Chicago to Greensboro, she moved with us. She came into the Greensboro plant and worked. She prayed, and the Lord continuously blessed us. I know now that without what she did for us, we wouldn't be here today. One day, I asked her, "Why did you do all this?"

She said, "I saw you in my mind, walking on Lake Shore Drive." She comes around now, from time to time, and she continues praying for us.

When you pray and have faith, God will help you either directly or by providing a way, or by sending someone who can help you. For me, God sent Mrs. Olivia Jackson—my Angel.

Distribution Rights to Fuller Products Acquired

I had a lot of responsibility, but not a lot of power when it came to implementing changes. Mr. Fuller was permitting distributors to get products on credit, and many of them were making no effort to pay the company back. As the bills stacked up, our electricity was disconnected, and we were unable to manufacture products. Eunice and I decided to buy the building and pay off the past-due utility bill. But we couldn't afford to keep bailing the company out of every financial hardship.

In December of 1983, we turned our thoughts to moving back to North Carolina, where our company had done so well. By the time we made up our minds to leave Chicago, there was a substantial amount of back rent due to us from Fuller Products. We realized that the company would probably never be able to repay us, so we chalked it up as our loss.

Eunice and I went to Mr. Fuller and proposed to buy exclusive rights to manufacture his products and use the Fuller name. Mr. Fuller trusted that Eunice and I would continue to carry out his mission, and we promised to do just that. We made a decison to be back in North Carolina by the Summer of 1984.

I believe to this day that had Eunice and I not accepted, in faith, Mr. Fuller's request to move to Chicago to run Fuller Products Company, Dudley Products Company would not have become the company that it is today. I also believe that God presented this challenge to us to prepare us to be able to help others become successful and to accept the responsibility to make a difference in the world.

Winning My Test of Faith

Al Gaddy
Dudley Route Sales Manager
New York City

I joined Fuller Products many years ago. I was there when the company was in its heyday and when it began to have financial problems. I recall that one day during a regular sales meeting, Mr. Dudley and Mr. Fuller petitioned all of us dealers for help. As soon as they brought up the topic of the company's financial standing, the room got quiet. This was the sort of thing none of us really wanted to talk about. Although I listened to everything they had to say, I imagine that I was not the only one thinking, "Oh boy, I've got to get out of this company and find more stable work."

I was confused about what impact these challenges would have on my job and my ability to earn a decent living. By the time they finished talking, something inside of me just kept saying, "Al, you cannot say you love and support this company but do nothing at a critical time like this." As the meeting drew to a close, I was feeling more and more like a hypocrite. Unable to shake that feeling, I approached Mr. Dudley and asked whether he had a few minutes to talk with me.

I told him I really wanted to help. I explained that although I genuinely cared about Fuller Products, quite frankly, I was scared about investing my money. I wanted some reassurance that my investment would not be lost. Mr. Dudley said that he could certainly understand my not wanting to lose the savings I had worked all my life to acquire. He also promised me that if I would support the company, neither he or Mr. Fuller would ever forget it. He said that he would personally strive to repay me, regardless of what happened with Fuller Products.

I invested my life's savings in the company. My decision marked the biggest test of faith I'd ever taken. And after I'd done it, my entire work ethic was changed. I stopped looking at work as simply an opportunity to make money. I took a real interest in the company, especially because my money was tied into it. Being a dealer became much more than just a job. I became consumed with the idea of setting a good example for the other dealers, so that they would work hard too. I wanted to see Fuller Products beat the odds. I've had no regrets about my decision to help.

Through faith, my personal concerns over finances have always managed to work themselves out. I have learned that there is no scarcity of resources as long as I listen to God and put my trust in Him. This experience made a big change in me. I am much more focused today on how I can help others. My interest is not just "What can I get out of this?" but "How can I help someone else?"

For as long as I've known him, Mr. Dudley has always lived out the principle of helping others. From his early days at Fuller Products, when most people were concerned with leading our internal competition for sales and recruiting, Mr. Dudley took time out to help other dealers. There is something different about him. But back then, I did not know what it was. Now, however, I know: Mr. Dudley is committed to empowering others.

CHAPTER 8

Don't Add Loss to Loss

Before we returned to North Carolina, Eunice and I decided to sell the office building in Chicago. We planned to use the money from the sale to build a new corporate office and manufacturing facility in Greensboro. It was during this time that I learned an important lesson about what I call *adding loss to loss.*

During the time I spent in Chicago, I had become very good friends with a man from that city. He was a wealthy man, and I respected him primarily because we seemed to share the same work ethic. We were neighbors in Glenview, where Eunice and I had built a home. Quite honestly, I was pleased to count this man among my short list of friends. I have always enjoyed the company of people who have made great accomplishments in their lives. They inspire me to greater activity in my own life. This man was no different. I saw admirable qualities in him.

When Eunice and I set our asking price for the building, my friend expressed an interest in buying it. I was pleasantly surprised by his interest and agreed to do all I could to facilitate the sale. We even discussed the possibility of my financing the building for him. Being cautious business people, we checked out his references and helped our real-estate agent obtain all of the necessary information. Everything seemed to be in place.

After the sale was negotiated, he defaulted on his payments. In fact, I learned that my friend had deceived me about several important facts. I had been cheated and, as you can guess, I was angry. I couldn't believe that a man I trusted so completely and believed to be my friend would actually treat me this way. But that's exactly what he did. Some people had tried to warn me about him, but I wouldn't hear of it. It seemed strange to me that the new windows I had installed in the building were mysteriously taken right out of the window frames.

We went to court, and the litigation dragged on for months. Even our house in Glenview was tied up in the lawsuit. He was trying to take that, too. We eventually got the equity out of our home, but keeping our office building was a bigger challenge.

Since we didn't have the money from the sale of the building or of our house to use as working capital toward a new facility, we were forced to settle for a lesser location in Greensboro. We signed a month-to-month lease and agreed to make do with the facility until we could resolve all of the legalities.

I was angry and frustrated at the legal system for causing us so many headaches. I had done nothing wrong; yet my money was being tied up anyway. I was extremely bitter about the whole situation, and my usually positive outlook on things was reduced to a state of negativity and complaining. I was even angry at myself for being so trustful of a person whom I really did not know at all. Why couldn't I see his true colors?, I kept thinking. I was full of stress over the possibility of losing something that I had worked hard to pay for. Something inside of me just kept eating away at my spirit.

Letting Go and Moving On

I picked up my copy of **Think and Grow Rich** and read for six straight hours. Afterward, I made a decision that shocked a lot of people, including my wife and family. I backed out of the lawsuit. Although it was a tough decision to make, I knew that I didn't have a choice. I could continue to fight it out in court, or I could put the whole mess behind me and get on with my life.

After making that decision, I felt as though a heavy weight had been lifted from my shoulders. I realized how big a burden the situation had been for me. To stay consumed in litigation that was taking years to resolve, I was only adding loss to loss—the potential loss of my building and home and, more important, the loss of my energy and enthusiasm. I knew that I couldn't afford to do that. I had to let go of the anger and focus solely on the here and now.

As it turned out, I was able to keep our house, but I lost the building. People would say, "Mr. Dudley, I heard you dropped the lawsuit and lost your building. You must be angry and devastated."

"No," I would respond, "I've let go of the anger. I know that I have to be grateful. Gratitude leads to plenty. Besides, I can get another building."

This Is How God Works

I started to illustrate my reasoning to our salespeople by taking a piece of paper and explaining it to them.

"Do you see this sheet of paper?" I asked. Then I continued: "Well, this full sheet represents the abundance that God promises us. God will give you a little bit . . . ," and I tore off a piece of the sheet, ". . . then he will give you more . . . ," and I tore off a slightly bigger piece. "Then God will give you even more . . ." I tore off a bigger piece. "Then God will take away some of what he has given you, through some challenge, to test your gratefulness and faith . . . ," and I removed the second piece I had torn off. "We may not have done anything wrong, but if we get angry and start complaining, it shows God that we aren't truly grateful. We're saying that we don't even care about the portion that remains. When that happens, God may take away even more . . . ," and I removed the third piece I had torn. "But if we are grateful, as Job was, for the part we still have; if we refuse to harbor anger and spite; then God will give us what we lost (I replaced the second and third pieces) and give us more than ever before," and I put the rest of the original sheet with the torn pieces.

"So you see, that's how I feel about the whole situation with my losing the building. I'm not going to spend my life being bitter and complaining about what has happened. Instead, I'm going to be grateful for the wonderful things I still have. In time, God will bless me with another building, a building that is much better than the one I lost."

I learned from that experience that life is a package deal. It comes with a fair share of gains and setbacks. Sometimes it's better to forfeit the fight than it is to keep at it. Sometimes, the fight alone can do you more harm than the end result. By jeopardizing your positive, grateful spirit for the sake of fighting, you're only adding loss to loss.

Don't Add Loss to Loss
(A Tribute to Mr. Joe Louis Dudley, Sr.)

When subtracting the joy
From the pain,
It adds up to a gift of spirit
No one can explain.

Come what may,
Nobody's born to lose;
As long as you're living,
The choice is yours to choose.

A man with the knowledge,
The wisdom, and the will
Is a man with the Fuller spirit
And a faith made of steel.

No matter what people might say,
Today is tomorrow yesterday;
And no matter what the cost,
Don't add loss to loss.

To live and love
In a Fuller state of mind
Is to give of yourself,
One day at a time.

118

Don't Add Loss to Loss

In the light of divine order,
Any lost cause can be found,
And because of the inner you,
You know there's a higher ground.

To make you feel brand new
Is to fill your loving cup,
So the gift of a good challenge
Can show you which way is up.

Don't live your life
On what was way back when;
Pick yourself up, and you can
Soar to sweet success again.

No matter what people might say,
Today was tomorrow yesterday;
And no matter what the cost,
Don't add loss to loss.

—Daniel R. Queen
Copyright 1989
All Rights Reserved

Family

Age 17, attending S. W. Snowden High School (1954).

Starting to sell Fuller products at age 20 to help pay my college tuition (1957).

Engagement picture of Eunice and me (1960).

Family photo with Eunice, Joe Jr., Ursula, and Genea (1993).

My parents' dream is fulfilled and all 11 children graduate from college (1976).
Juarez D. Little Photographer

Wedding picture of my parents, Gilmer and Clara Yeates Dudley (1929).

Joe Jr. and I accepted leadership positions in American Health and Beauty Aids Institute (AHBAI) Joe Jr. as Chair of Operations and I served as chairman of the AHBAI Board (1995).

My mother and 10 siblings enjoying our annual family reunion (1996).
Natalie Bennett Photographer

Ursula and Mark Oglesby wedding.
© *1996 Larry Yow Photography*

The house my parents, grandfather, siblings, and I once lived in as a child.

Ballam D. Dudley, (1858–1971) my grandfather born a slave, sitting with his son, Uncle W. K., holding my son, Joe Jr.

Yeates Convention Center a monument to honor my mother, Mrs. Clara Yeates Dudley (1994).

The 20-Room Kernersville, NC Mansion Eunice and I call home (1988).

"Without my mother's belief, I might not have realized my dreams. As a first grader with a speech impediment, I was labeled mentally retarded. But my mother, Clara Yeates Dudley, believed in me and continued to challenge me. My mother told me to prove them wrong." – *Mr. Joe L. Dudley Sr.*

My mother, Mrs. Clara Yeates Dudley, who challenged me to "Fool Them and Prove Them Wrong" (1993).

With Eunice and my father, Gilmer Dudley at O'Hare Airport Chicago (1966).

Fuller Products Co. Related

peaking at Mr. S. B. Fuller's 70th birthday cel-
bration in Chicago, Mr. Johnson Ebony/Jet is
hown to my left (1975).

Mr. Fuller and I after my acceptance of presidency
of Fuller Products Company position (1976).

The Don't Add Loss to Loss" building I once owned in
hicago (1984).

Greeting Fuller door to door sales personnel (Louie Corpening, Mrs. Mary Shanklin,
and Mrs. Mimi Anderson) 1979.

Learning Fuller Branch Management from Mr. John Johnson. Brooklyn Branch Manager (1960).

The "Angel" God sent to me, Mrs. Olivia Jackson, addresses Dudley year-end sales meeting (1990).

Staff and sales team from our 30 Macon Street branch in Brooklyn (1982).
George Thomas, photographer

John H. Johnson (Ebony/Jet) and George Johnson (Johnson Products) disciples of Mr. S. B. Fuller's Entrepreneurial Message present a bust to him at 70th birthday celebration (1975).

Mr. S. B. Fuller addresses attendees at his 70th birthday celebration at the Chicago Conrad Hilton Hotel (1975).

Eunice and I present a new Cadillac to Mr. Fuller for his 80th birthday (1985).

Dan Walker, then Governor of Illinois, presents Proclamation to Mr. S. B. Fuller on his 70th birthday (1975).

Jim Thompson, Governor of Illinois, and his wife pay a visit to Fuller Products 63rd Street office. Also shown L-R Rev. Richard Collins (wrote poem: No Time To Play.) Mrs. Mary Wilkins, Mrs. Julia Futrell, next to Miss Thompson, and Ms. Phyllis Stapler (1978).

George Thomas, photographer

Mr. Fuller's 70th birthday celebration. Mr. Samuel Dicks, far right, strong force in development of Fuller Products, and from left to right: Mrs. Scroggins, Mary Dubose, Mae West, Sylvia Morrison, and Mr. Roosevelt Hall (1975).

Fuller Distributors Get Together; First row (sitting L-R) Mrs. Carlos, Mrs. Tina Tarver, and Mrs. Earline Scroggins. Second row (Standing L-R) Henry Tarver, Charles McSwain, Lucious Woods, Joe Knight, Archer Greg, and Alfred Dudley, Sr. (1974).

George Thomas, photographer

Dudley Products, Inc. Development

With Eunice, Neville Evans, and Terrie Clawson at new headquarters ground breaking ceremony (1993).

Dr. Bobby Jones and I announcing the "Dudley Moments" association with BET (1993).

Presenting my brother Alfred with the Dudley Products, Inc. Top Salesman Award (1990).

Dudley's new corporate head-quarters and manufacturing complex (1994).

Addressing Dudley morning reading session (1996).

Staff members
attending daily
reading session
(1996).

Personally congratulating a new
DCU Advanced Class Graduate
(1994).

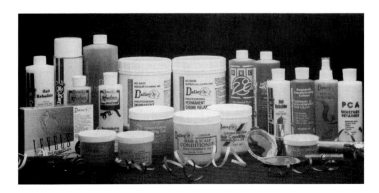

Group shot
of Dudley
produced
items.

During year-end sales meeting in the Bahamas (1988).

Dudley's 1st corporate office and plant we built located next to Route-40 in Greensboro (1986).

Dudley Cosmetology University, Kernersville, NC, The "Cosmetology Capital of the World" (1989).

Dudley's DCU Inn and Travel Agency . . . Serving students and the public (1992).

DCU Basic
School students.

A DCU Advanced
Class graduation
photo (1992).

Representative-NC,
Mel Watt offers con-
gratulations at luncheon
for President Mugabe
(1994).

Dudley demonstration stage at Bronner Bros. Atlanta show (1993).

Addressing an open session during the Greensboro Educational Motivation Seminar Event (1993).

Photo of Chicago sales and office team (1981).

Awards & Recognition Events

Looking on as Laska Jones, a long-time Dudley employee makes a humorous point at a sales meeting (1987).

Cecil Rouson addresses Dudley sales banquet (1990).

Dudley Fellows meet Representative Howard Coble at the Capitol (1991).

Dudley Products is honored to have Mrs. Rosa Parks civil rights legend visit (1995).

Chatting with the legendary Mary Kay Ash of Mary Kay Cosmetics and entertainer Helen Goldsby at Horatio Alger Association Induction (1995).

Eunice and I were honored and pleased to have the late Betty Shabazz attend our event to honor President Mugabe of Zimbabwe (1995).

Fellow Horatio Alger members: Dr. Robert Schuller, George L. Argyros, Herschel Walker, and I after the induction ceremony (1995).

Receiving the Horatio Alger Award from my very good friend Mr. Bob Brown of B&C Associates (1995).

Dave Thomas, founder of Wendy's offers thanks for my participating in his Enterprise Ambassador Program's Only in America Conference (1996).

Dudley Products Inc., Dudley Fellows Program is recognized by President George Bush with his 467th Point of Light Award (1991).

On-stage with poet/author Maya Angelou supporting UNCF Telethon (1992).

Receiving an Honorary Doctorate from my Alma Mater, North Carolina A&T State University (1991).

Special Programs

Eunice and I along with staff accepting The Direct Selling Association Vision For Tomorrow Award for Dudley Fellows Program (1991).

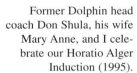

Former Dolphin head coach Don Shula, his wife Mary Anne, and I celebrate our Horatio Alger Induction (1995).

Dudley Products, Inc. were grateful sponsors of The Black Teenage World Pageant for a number of years (1992).

Eunice and I chatting with George Johnson (Johnson Products), Dr. Johnny Coleman, and Dr. Lewis Baskins.

Betty Sharpe (DCU) explains activities at the Basic School to President Mugabe during visit to Kernersville (1995).

Shown at Direct Selling Association Meeting with Frank and Jan Day of Jafra Cosmetics (1991).

North Carolina Governor Hunt and I met with African business people (1994).

Discussing assistance opportunities with his Excellency Robert Mugabe of Zimbabwe during his visit to Kernersville (1995).

Hosting Dudley Collegiate Program participants in Florida (1996).

John Raye (left) and Dr. Willie Bailey, my Mastermind Alliance and developers of The Dudley Collegiate Sales Program (1995).

North Carolina Governor James Hunt extends an invitation to accompany him to Africa. Looking on, left to right, are Terrie Clawson, Director of Dudley International-South America, Bob Brown of B&C Associates, and Betty Clawson, Director of the Dudley Beauty College-Chicago (1994).

Joanie Hayes, Director of International-Africa, shares the Dudley Vision with a Cosmetology Class at Zimbabwe's Chinoyi Technical School (1995).

Here I am attending a very spirited meeting of cosmetology students from Zimbabwe (1996).

CHAPTER 9

Be Committed and Concerned

With the loss of my building a thing of the past, I set out on a new mission. We planned to increase distribution of our products significantly. We promoted a number of our salespeople to the professional route. They marketed our products exclusively to hair salons and licensed professionals. Other salespeople were assigned residential territories, which they enthusiastically canvassed, selling the Fuller Products line of personal-care items.

Building Sales Commitment and Concerns

In keeping with Mr. Fuller's philosophy that image is important, our salespeople were required to wear business attire when they worked. We spent many hours learning to think positively and developing postive attitudes. At every sales meeting, I reminded the sales managers that servicing a customer's needs and doing it well involves much more than merely dropping off products and picking up money. It requires personal commitment if you want to achieve wealth, success, and personal fulfillment through sales.

Initially, the newcomers to our company didn't take me seriously. I heard their comments about changing times and my old-fashioned approach to selling. I knew that they were more motivated by dollars and cents, so I constantly preached to them that, without some measure of commitment and concern about their customers, the money would stop coming in.

Leading By Example

Once, to prove a point, I volunteered to work a sales route for 90 days. I told the salespeople that I could outsell any one of them. There was a lot of murmuring about the challenge. Some people halfheartedly joked that I was in for a rude awakening. But I fooled them all. As it turned out, 95% of the people I approached made a purchase. In just two days, I had sold more products than the average salesperson did in one week. Every week during the 90-day period, my sales increased. I know that it did not happen by accident. It happened because I showed more interest in my customers and their futures than I did in how much money they spent on my products. I talked with them about becoming self-sufficient, and gave them new ideas about increasing revenue in their businesses. I wasn't just selling products; I was selling hope. I proved to all of the salespeople that my approach, as old-fashioned as it may have seemed, was still the best.

Growing and Rewarding the Sales Force

Over the next two years, building Dudley Products remained my number-one goal. Eunice and I managed to recruit even more loyal, determined salespeople. We hired people who had the potential to do a variety of jobs. As a growing company, we had to be as efficient as possible. Everybody on our staff wore more than one hat. Sales began to climb, and our market grew larger. Our annual sales soared again.

Out of gratitude to the employees who had helped make it all possible, Eunice and I played host to our first year-end conference. We went to Southern California and took everybody along. We had a wonderful time and, as a result, each year my wife continued the tradition of planning our year-end conference at different exotic locations. We've been to Hawaii, Florida, Jamaica, Cancun, and the Bahamas. I'll admit that in the beginning, financing these trips was tough. But each year, we made the reservations on faith, trusting that we would be able to pay the bill when the time came.

Once, as we neared the conclusion of our conference at a very elegant hotel, our accountant told me that we didn't have enough money to pay the hotel. As soon as I told everyone what was going on, our sales managers hit the streets, going door to door, selling the only product we had left in stock—Dudley's Aloe Vera Night Cream. Within a few hours, they had earned enough money for us to settle the bill and leave. That's teamwork in action! These days, we look back and laugh about that experience.

Black Businesses Working Together

As our professional sales increased, my commitment to our partnership with cosmetologists intensified. I became more outspoken in my support of the beauty industry, especially within the African-American community. I sought opportunities to work with other professionals in the field. I joined the American Health and Beauty Aids Institute (AHBAI) in Chicago.

This organization is made up of manufacturers and distributors of African-American health and beauty aids for professionals, including Soft Sheen, Luster Products, Bronner Brothers, Afam Concepts, Kizure Products, and A. W. Curtis Laboratories. Several of these business owners had come up through the same trenches I had. Each of our business experiences had some common threads. I could count on them for encouragement and advice, and they could rely on me for the same.

My very good friend, Jerry White, owner of Kizure Products, is an excellent example of how determination, perseverance, and working together with others leads to success. Jerry and his wife, Lucky, have been friends with Eunice and me for well over 25 years. We have also purchased products from Kizure for about that length of time. The four of us have traveled together to places such as South Africa and Hong Kong.

If you have an opportunity to read or hear the career-development story of Jerry and Lucky, you cannot help but be inspired. By his own account, he has been bankrupt many times and has lost more than seven cars and three homes. Yet, despite all these obstacles and distractions, he has become a leading inventor of heat products for hair servicing. He has invented stoves, hot combs, and other products sold not only by us but also by many other companies in the hair-care industry. He was also a pioneer in recognizing the opportunities in nail care long before the current efforts.

Jerry and Lucky, for the past few years, have been building a $10-million-dollar home in California on a self-financed pay-as-you-go basis. Jerry also recently fulfilled a lifetime dream by completing his high-school requirements, and earning his GED.

Jerry and Lucky's support and friendship have really meant a lot to Eunice and me, along with many other friendships. Their success is due in part to their determination and perseverance, and to their helping and working with others.

We all are dedicated to the philosophy of investing in the communities that support our businesses. We strive to provide both monetary assistance and economic empowerment through job creation, mentoring, and education. In 1994, Albany, Georgia, experienced severe flooding that left many people without homes and businesses. The executive director of AHBAI, Geri Duncan Jones, told the member companies about the plight of the cosmetologists in Albany. Some salons were badly damaged, and others were completely destroyed.

Geri asked us to take an active role in helping the cosmetologists in that area. Each member company donated products and money to the cause. The staff at AHBAI and a few entertainment celebrities went to Albany and presented the cosmetologists there with more than $35,000 worth of products.

AHBAI has also been instrumental in donating more than $250,000 to the United Negro College Fund as well as more than

$125,000 to a variety of scholarship programs benefiting young people. In 1995, I was named chairman of the board of directors at AHBAI.

AHBAI Annual Entrepreneur Leadership Conference

Later that year, Dudley Products served as the host site for AHBAI's first annual Entrepreneur Leadership Conference and $25,000 scholarship program.

We got in touch with students at each of the historically black colleges and universities in America. We asked them to write essays on the subject of entrepreneurship and leadership. The winners from each school were then invited to attend the conference, at which they could meet business leaders and skilled entrepreneurs. Members of AHBAI include Al Washington, *AFAM Concepts, Inc/SAG;* Ernest Joshua, *J M Products, Inc.;* Jerry White, *Kizure Professional Products;* Clyde Hammond, *Summit Laboratories, Inc.;* Russ Little, Jr., *Afro World Hair Co.;* Austin W. Curtis, *A. W. Curtis Laboratories;* Bernard Bronner, *Bronner Bros.;* Nathaniel Bronner, *Bronner Bros.;* Chapman Cannon, *Southwest American Mfg. Co., Inc.;* Comer Cottrell, *Pro-line Corporation;* Edward Garner, *Soft Sheen Products, Inc.;* Harry Green, *Green Acre, Inc.;* Cyrus Jackson, *Professional Products Unlimited, Inc.;* Rudolphus Johnson, *Pride & Power, Inc.;* Jory Luster, *Luster Products, Inc.;* Cornell McBride, *McBride Research Laboratories;* H. R. Phillips, *High Time Products, Inc.;* Charles Young, Sr., *E. F. Young Mfg. Co.;* and Joe L. Dudley, Sr., *Dudley Products, Inc.*

Students were free to ask questions and learn more about how a variety of people had gotten their starts in business. The conference concluded with our awarding a total of $25,000 in scholarship money.

AHBAI is committed to the industry, and I gladly support its mission. In a very real sense, the cosmetology industry represents one of only a few permanent businesses that can be traced to African-American communities throughout the country.

Ever since Madam C. J. Walker showed us in 1905 how the pressing comb could be converted into cash flow, the field of cosmetology has blossomed into more than a billion-dollar-a-year industry, providing thousands of jobs and business opportunities in the African-American Community. (Source: Dudley's Haircare Fact Book, 1993). Likewise, hair salons and sellers of ethnic beauty aids make a tremendous impact in their communities by giving back.

Millions of dollars are lost on a regular basis because of our inability to understand the buying power of our dollars. Too many people are uneducated about the fact that where they spend money is where they develop and enhance business and employment opportunities. At one time, African-American hair-care manufacturers dominated the ethnic hair-care market, but now they have relinquished a significant portion of that control to non-African-American companies. If this trend continues at the rate we're currently going, it will lead to the collapse of what is one of the most profitable industries in Black America.

We are facing many challenges, and the stakes are high; but we can win if we work hard.

And that is what we strive to do at Dudley Products. We take our partnership with the professional cosmetologist very seriously, and we align ourselves with others who share our passion. When there is a cause or mission that you feel passionately about, it's always a good idea to join forces with others who share your interest. Whether it's a support group or a civic organization, you will benefit from the combined forces of several people. Often it's easier to accomplish significant goals when a collective energy is at work. Seek out people who can work with you to make a real difference in the world.

You Can Come Home Again and Again

Roy Williams
Director
Dudley Beauty School
Bennettsville, South Carolina

I know all too well the importance of the statement, "You can al-ways go home." I came to work with Mr. Dudley in 1967, shortly af-ter he opened a Fuller distributorship in Greensboro. At that time, I employed a crew of almost 50 door-to-door salespeople. They sold a variety of products for different manufacturers, including cosmetic and hair-care companies. Mr. Dudley came to see me one day and discussed the possibility of using my sales force to distribute his products.

When he began to talk about his mission and goals, I was im-pressed, but not quite as drawn to the concept of raising people as I was to raising the balance in my bank account. Mr. Dudley invited me to go to Atlanta one weekend for a Fuller Products sales confer-ence. During the conference, I participated in a number of meetings and seminars. Everyone made me feel like a part of their company.

On the drive back, I told the Dudleys that I liked Mr. Fuller's views on economic empowerment and self-sufficiency. I also admired the fact that the company had more lofty goals than just making money. Still, I added, I'll need a few days to think it over.

Eventually, my sales crew became agents for the Dudley's dis-tributorship. We attended regular sales meetings, at which Mr. Dud-

127

*ley impressed upon all of us the company's philosophies. He in-
spired us to be excited and to sell products with enthusiasm.*

*But I was not interested in assuming a salesman's role. I had
spent a number of years in a wheelchair, and although I had re-
gained the ability to walk, I had a limp that made me very self-
conscious. Mr. Dudley would often tell me that the best way to overcome my anxiety about the way I walked was to get out there and
face my fear. He really wanted me to try door-to-door selling, but I
just wouldn't do it. In fact, I got angry with him every time he mentioned it. He just wouldn't take no for an answer.*

*After a few years, I was offered a job with a manufacturing co-
op in Virginia that promised me a good salary. Out of respect, I went
to Mr. Dudley and told him that I couldn't pass up the opportunity to
earn more money. He understood my decision to leave and wished
me the best of luck. Some time later, I returned to Dudley Products
after being fired from the co-op. Mr. Dudley said, "Welcome home,
Roy. Let's just put the past behind us and start all over."*

*With that, I resumed my job, and even tried door-to-door selling
in the evenings. It wasn't long before I got the itch for more money.
This time, I decided to open a janitorial services company. I told Mr.
Dudley that some of my sales crew would also be leaving. He accepted my resignation, but cautioned me about pulling my salespeople out of the company.*

*"They're doing well here," he told me, "but what's going to hap-
pen if your business doesn't work out?"*

*I didn't really think about the impact it might have on the oth-
ers, because I didn't plan to fail this time around.*

*However, a few years later, that business folded. Some of the
salespeople went back to work for Mr. Dudley, but not me. I had too
much pride. I was too embarrassed to even call Mr. Dudley and tell
him what had happened. One day, in 1982, I was in a local hard-
ware store and ran into one of the people who used to work for me.
He was glad to see me, and told me that Mr. Dudley often asked how
I was doing. He suggested that I stop by to visit him.*

Be Committed and Concerned

I met Mr. Dudley one night for dinner, and we caught up on what was going on in our lives. I told him that my latest business venture had soured. "Not only that," I said, "but my wife has divorced me, and the lenders are threatening to foreclose on my house."

Mr. Dudley asked me why I hadn't just come back to the company.

"I was just too embarrassed and ashamed," I said.

Mr. Dudley told me about his move to Chicago to assume the presidency at Fuller Products. He asked me to consider coming with him. I agreed. Again, I assumed a role in the company, this time doing quite a bit of door-to-door sales. I became comfortable with selling. My walking improved, and people who hadn't known me before didn't even notice my limp. I also met my current wife, Audrey Jean, while in Chicago. She, too, worked for the company.

I stayed with Dudley Products from 1982 to 1994. Then I convinced my wife that we should resign and start our own business. One year later, on Christmas Eve, Mr. Dudley called to wish us a Merry Christmas. I suspect that he had heard we were more than $240,000 in debt, although he never said it. Instead, he said, "Roy, I don't know what you're doing right now, but I've been wondering whether you and Audrey would consider coming back to Dudley Products."

In two days, I returned his call with the news that Audrey and I were coming home to Dudley Products. Four times I left the company, and four times I came back. I am convinced that there is no employer in the world who would have tolerated me for so long. No one that is, except for Mr. Dudley.

As I write this, I am 50 years old, but I have assured Mr. Dudley that I've got 50 more years to go. I'm so glad to be back home that I've put myself on a 50-year plan of improvement. And this time, I'm going to do it the Dudley Way.

Yes, You Sure Can Come Home Again!

Raymond Terry
Dudley Route Sales Manager

My parents were Jehovah's Witnesses, so every week we went door to door, distributing magazines and books, trying to persuade people to have Bible studies with us.

Around the time of my junior year in high school, my relationship with my father became strained. I asked too many questions about his religion, and I wanted to go to college. Since he believed the world was going to end in a few years, college was out of the question. So two weeks after graduating from high school, I had a job, my own apartment, and was enrolled in college at night.

*While studying in the library, I stumbled across a book on white-collar crime (**How to Steal With a Pen**). It talked about the crimes people committed, how much money they made, and how they got away with it. Wow! In our community, black men were getting caught committing petty crimes and doing large time. I studied every book on white-collar crime and criminology I could find.*

This took me almost a year to get going. Following exactly what I read, within 18 months I was earning $2,000 per week and training three recruits on my system. They would keep half the money and I would keep half. My goal was to spread across the country, opening businesses teaching people how to steal with a pen.

Fortunately, or unfortunately, I was almost arrested for trying to cash a check in my crooked brother-in-law's name. At the time, I had

Be Committed and Concerned

$2,000 in checks and three fake licenses on me. For some reason I was never searched. That seemed to be a sign for me. My plan had been to free black people, including me, from poverty. Going to jail never crossed my mind until that day.

About a year later, after spending all the money I had made, I went to work for Fuller Products, selling cosmetics door-to-door. I prayed to God for a job where I could be free and help my people.

I met Mr. Dudley in New York at a sales meeting. He invited me to come to Chicago and train to be a manager, and I accepted. Within a couple of years, my future wife, Janice, and I were living on the 33rd floor of a high rise on Lake Shore Drive with two new cars. Living large, working hard.

A short while later, I collapsed and spent much time recovering from an illness. In one month, I lost about 40 pounds. My kidneys hurt; my chest hurt; all I could do was lie in bed. Janice finally persuaded me to go to the hospital, and I was admitted. For 22 days they could not find what was wrong with me. They thought I had a contagious disease. Everyone who came in contact with me had to wear gloves, masks, and gowns, which were burned after their visit. My third doctor decided to drill a small hole in my chest and do an examination. That was very depressing to me.

Mr. Dudley called me sometime during that day. He said he was in a meeting in New York, but he wanted to see how I was doing. He told me that whatever happens, if I say, "I AM, I CAN, and I WILL," everything would be all right.

That night I was out of it. The nurse had changed my bed and clothes twice, and they were not happy about it. I remember lying there in that bed soaking wet, my spirit ready to leave my body, thinking about what Mr. Dudley told me that day. Whatever happens, if I say, "I AM, I CAN, and I WILL," everything's going to be all right. I don't know why, but I just believed what he said. I said "I AM, I CAN, and I WILL, I AM, I CAN, and I WILL, I AM, I CAN, and I WILL," over and over again. "I AM, I CAN, AND I WILL." I said it from ten minutes to midnight until three in the morning. And I knew that everything was going to be all right.

The next day, my doctor told me they had discovered what was wrong with me and that I was going to be discharged the next day. My spirit laughed and danced and shouted.

My body healed in about nine months, but my mind was still depressed. One of the reasons for my sickness, I believe, was my attitude toward Mr. Dudley. I was mad at him because he said something in a meeting that I thought was negative toward me and indicated he was going to break a promise made to me. So I quit working for Dudley Products. My body was there, but my mind and spirit weren't.

I was in a bitter, contemptuous state of mind. It's impossible to sell products for a person you mistrust, so I finally quit.

For months, I looked for a job in sales, without finding one. We were broke, and I couldn't pay the rent on our two-room apartment. Janice was still in touch with Mr. Dudley who, hearing of our situation, would give her some products to sell and try to persuade her to convince me that I should come see him.

I finally found two jobs, cooking pasta in a pizza restaurant and selling World Book encyclopedias over the phone. Still, I couldn't get Dudley Products out of my mind. I thought about Mr. Dudley every day and blamed him for my ruined career and life. Mad and depressed, I picked up an old habit—drinking beer. Sitting, drinking my Miller High Life one evening, I decided to call "Old Joe Dudley" and give him a piece of the little mind I had left. So I did. Every time he tried to say something, I told him what he was going to tell me. I tried my best to irritate him, but he just stayed calm and laughed at me. He knew he was talking to a fool. Finally he hung up on me and I went back to living the "High Life."

One day, Janice persuaded me to go to the Dudley factory. Mr. Dudley was having a meeting. There was a person there named Roy Williams talking about how he worked for Dudley Products and got upset and quit. He said he started a business, lost it, lost his home and his wife, and almost became a bum on the street. That got my attention.

Be Committed and Concerned

Mr. Dudley persuaded me to tell my story, which I did. Everything came pouncing out of me. The bitterness and frustration of the last year. My mistrust of him and the company. Living on $7 worth of groceries per week. Losing my car, my health, my business, and my home. When I finished, I was born again. I was a new man with a new spirit. Cleansed. Washed whole.

That night, we went to Mr. Dudley's house and watched the "The Life of Paul."

Roy Williams became my best friend. We traveled together doing whatever Mr. Dudley asked for about a year. I now work in Boston, Mass., with a great business, a new wife and baby, and a great attitude about life. I'm grateful for the life I have, and I'm looking forward to a great future.

10

Let Faith Move Your Mountain

One evening in early 1986, around 10:15 p.m., about 45 people gathered with my wife and me on a densely wooded stretch of land. There, with only the illumination of street lights from the neighboring highway, we busied ourselves picking up trash and clearing debris from the land. As we went about our task, I felt a great sense of to-getherness. These people where employees of our company. They had left the comfort of their homes to come out and meet Eunice and me that evening. After about 30 minutes, I asked everbody to gather in a circle. We held hands, and I began to pray aloud.

We were standing on the site where my wife and I hoped to build a new corporate office and manufacturing facility. It had taken us months to find a suitable location, and we both agreed that this space seemed right. What we liked most about this land was its visibility from the highway. We could give inspiration to thousands of people, especially youth, who passed by and saw our headquarters from the interstate. We envisioned all the people who would say to themselves, as they drove by our facility, "Gee, if the Dudleys can build something like that, then I can too."

By meeting on the land that night to pray, we were stepping out on faith that it would one day be the site of our corporate headquar-ters and manufacturing plant. The Bible says that where two or more gather together in agreement, God is in their midst. We wanted God to know that we were serious in our endeavor. Hoping to set a strong example for others, we considered getting this building as a way to accomplish that.

We went to several banks and lenders to apply for financing. Although we found someone interested in financing our project, there was one stipulation. The lender could not finance both the cost of the land and the cost of construction; therefore, we were required to have full ownership of the land before we could borrow money toward construction costs. We were given three months to sell enough products to purchase the land. Again giving credence to the fact that when you walk by faith, things somehow manage to fall into place, one of our employees came up with the idea to start a campaign in honor of my wife's birthday.

The First Lady's Birthday Campaign

We called it just that, "The First Lady's Birthday Campaign." Our sales managers were asked to meet preset goals as a tribute to Mrs. Dudley, the chief financial officer of our company. We planned a special celebration for the sales managers who reached their goals.

After reading so much about how appreciative we are of our employees and how grateful and blessed we feel to have such loyal and dedicated people in our company, do you have any doubt that we raised enough money to buy the land? I sure hope not. Because true to Dudley style, we did it. Amid a lot of skepticism and doubt from outsiders, we overcame yet another challenge in the history of our company.

Mrs. Dudley's birthday campaign ended in February, the month of her birthday, and we cut a check to buy the land. In March, construction was under way. One of our employees, Laska Jones, went to the site frequently and videotaped the construction as it took form. On Tuesday nights, we gathered with our employees to view the tapes. Sales managers in other parts of the country were sent tapes as well, so that they felt a part of what was going on. We were all amazed at how the barren stretch of land was transformed into a beautiful office building. Then my wife began to work expeditiously with designers to make sure every detail of the building interior was just as beautiful.

McCloud Road Grand Opening

When the building was ready for occupancy, we planned our big grand opening celebration for December 29, 1986. Dressed in our best formal attire, and having the spirit and enthusiasm to match, we threw an extravagant party. It was the sort of event you see on television. It was a very formal affair. My wife wore a dress design originally created for the soap opera character *Erica Kane,* played by Susan Lucci, on *All My Children.* The gentlemen wore their best tuxedos. We had valet parking for our guests and a catered menu of exquisite foods, including caviar. Our invitation list was also first-rate. Dignitaries and friends from all over the country attended. Everyone was all smiles, and the testimonials they shared were packed with showings of support for Dudley Products Company. When I was finally given the opportunity to speak, I made it clear that our purpose that night was not to celebrate anything we had personally accomplished, but to glorify God for all the blessings we had received. Our faith in God had made this mission a reality.

We loved working in our new facility. The McCloud Road office represented a big milestone for us. It placed our company on the map, so to speak. People could associate our name with the beautiful building just off of Interstate 40 in Greensboro.

We weren't sure exactly how we would use all of its space, but we knew that it offered us plenty of room to grow. And that's exactly what we did. We added several new departments, such as marketing, customer satisfaction, and accounting. For the first time in our business life, specific people had specific responsibilities. Although we gave our employees a lot of independence and freedom to introduce improvements in our company, gone were the days when all the work rested on just a few people.

It didn't take long before we were using every available square foot of space in our building. After about six years, we were faced with the challenge of looking for additional office space. We spent many hours thinking about which departments of our company could function efficiently if relocated from the corporate office. Could we move the sales division? The customer services department? Making the right decison was very difficult. We eventually moved to our current Kernersville location.

Looking Toward Kernersville

We wanted to start a school for cosmetologists again, and initially we looked in Greensboro. Our friend and financial planner, Jim Corlett, told Eunice and me about some land for sale in the neighboring small town of Kernersville. Kernersville is strategically situated between the larger cities of Winston-Salem and Greensboro. It is an up-and-coming area where two-career couples live because of its convenience to larger business communities. Kernersville is a small community excellently located in the Triad area of North Carolina. It provides a very wholesome business environment.

One day, Eunice and I decided to drive over and look at the land. It was only about ten minutes from our McCloud Road location in Greensboro. The land was a heavily wooded area. Previously it was the site of Wesleyan Academy, a seminary turned private school for boys that closed in 1981. The land had been purchased by another manufacturing company, AMP, Inc., but AMP had done nothing to redevelop the site. The grounds of the former academy included classrooms, an auditorium, and dormitory space. However, what remained was the framework of several old and dilapidated buildings. Over the next few weeks, Eunice and I talked about the potential of the land. We saw beyond the work to be done and became convinced that it would make a wonderful location for our company.

138

The Substance of Things Hoped for

We took some of our employees with us to look at the land. We were eager to know what they thought of it.

"It's just lovely, isn't it?" said Eunice.

But no one said anything. It was pretty obvious to us that they didn't share our vision of the land. It took a few minutes for them to respond, and when they did, their only comment was, "Well, we obviously don't see what the two of you do, Mr. Dudley."

Because I wanted them to share in our excitement about the potential we saw, I told them all the things we envisioned happening on the land. We encouraged them not to look at the land through their human eyes, but to believe in faith that we could accomplish much more than what seemed possible. Eunice and I were seeing this wooded territory of old buildings as the world's newest cosmetology haven. Sure, it would require a lot of time and money to turn our dreams into reality, but we knew that with faith, all things are possible.

"Have you ever really wanted something so bad that you were willing to do whatever it took to get it?" I asked them. "Well, that's how Eunice and I felt about this land."

I told them that when you set a goal toward something you really want, your vision about getting it is clear. You cannot stop thinking about the thing until it happens. Your metabolism increases, and your adrenaline rushes every time you get a step closer to your dream. There is no feeling that quite compares to the exhilaration of going after a coveted goal. And that's how we were feeling about the land.

Eunice and I met with our financial advisor to find out what we needed to do to buy the land. He worked with us on getting our finances in shape. This time around, we didn't want any stipulations or conditions on our financing package. Mr. Corlett advised us of all the concerns the banks might have about financing our deal. He told us that we had several assets that could be liquidated and used as working capital. If we decided to let go of some of these things, we wouldn't be dependent on a lender for the total purchase price of the land and the construction costs.

From there, Eunice and I discussed which assets we were willing to sell. We had to take a serious look at our long-range objectives. We were taking a chance on ourselves and our company. But we had faith. We believed that if we sold any of our personal assets, we would eventually make the money back and come out ahead. Although the decisions were difficult to make, we were hopeful. Eunice said, "Joe, there have been many times when we were on the verge of bankruptcy, but we never filed. Our faith has always worked to our advantage."

We talked about all the money we had invested in Fuller Products, which cost us so much of our personal savings. Although we could have been justified in filing bankruptcy, we never did. We had faith and we went to work. It was a formula that we knew worked.

We did a spring cleaning of all our assets and decided which to keep and which to let go. It was a refreshing experience, one that I readily encourage others to do. If an investment is costing you more money than it's worth, let it go. Sell it or convert it to a more beneficial use. What might have been a good investment a few years ago may not be the best choice for you today. And, most important, you sometimes have to sacrifice a little to gain a little more. This certainly worked for Eunice and me.

One investment we held on to was the building that houses the Dudley Beauty School in Washington, D.C. We purchased this building in 1990 through the efforts and assistance of my brother Cornelius, who had office space in the building. This purchase and the school itself made Dudley a player in the beauty-education industry. Cornelius' assistance was instrumental in this development. He has tremendous experience in purchasing and acquiring real estate. He invested wisely while employed in the United States Navy as an electrical engineer, and currently operates and manages his own multimillion-dollar real-estate properties.

Launching of Dudley Cosmetology University (DCU)

In December 1988, we paid about $2 million for the 54 acres of land in Kernersville. We renovated the buildings one by one. We started out with a parcel of land and a burning desire to open a school. Dudley Cosmetology University (DCU) opened its doors in April of the following year. We started with an advanced training program for professional cosmetologists. We offered a four-day program, from Sunday through Thursday, which taught a variety of advanced training techniques and specialty courses designed to help cosmetologists improve their skills.

Although not all the finishing touches were complete on the school when we opened, we had several students ready to enroll; so we started with what we had. A significant amount of money had already been spent, but we needed the revenue from student tuition to help us finish up. We set up our classroom in the auditorium, which was finished. We had an electrician put plugs all around the walls, so students would work from their stations. By the time our third class was enrolled, we had finished renovations of the Smith Building, which housed our Advanced Training program.

We developed a certificate program of study to keep licensed professionals ahead of hair-care and beauty-aid trends, and also to establish them as leaders in their field. We believed that cosmetologists, like other licensed professionals, should have an educational system whereby they might specialize in certain skills. The program is very structured and is recognized as the pinnacle of advanced education for cosmetologists. Certificate candidates exemplify professionals who are serious enough about their careers to want the highest level of certification offered. It has been stated that DCU is the "Harvard of Cosmetology Schools." If that's the case, then graduates of our advanced program are the best cosmetologists in the country.

By September 1989, we were ready to open our General School of Cosmetology for newcomers in the field. Those who finish the undergraduate program can receive certificates in basic cosmetology, manicuring, esthetics, and instructor training. There are additional seminars that focus on banking, customer service, financial planning, business management, and other important issues to self-employed individuals. These students remain in residence for an average of ten months. Many of the graduates of this program go on to become salon owners and managers, manicurists, estheticians, make-up artists, and cosmetology teachers.

Around the time we opened the General School, we also began operating a full-service cafeteria. Our primary objective was to provide nutritious meals at an affordable price for our students. The meal costs were built into their tuition. In additon, many of our employees and people from the community supported the cafeteria by coming in for breakfast and lunch.

Where Are We Going to House the Students?

As DCU grew in popularity, we became known as one of the leading schools of instruction for cosmetologists in the United States. With newer programs of study and an ever-increasing student population, we recognized the need for living quarters for our students in residence.

One of DCU's students had remarked to the press, "It's hard to find an apartment. Having a place to stay here on campus would mean so much. They already have food here. The cafeteria serves three meals a day; it's included in the tuition. It would be even easier if we could stay right here on campus, especially for those students who don't have access to a car."

Being attentive to her concerns and those of a majority of DCU's enrollees, Eunice and I agreed to build a hotel. As part of our long-range plan, we had already thought about opening a dormitory or hotel, but hearing their immediate concerns caused us to take action a lot sooner than we originally anticipated.

By 1991, after more than 5,000 cosmetologists from around the world had attended DCU, the timing was right. We hired Omni Architects of Charlotte, North Carolina, to design the building and Weaver Construction in Greensboro to build it. After the hotel was completed, DCU students and a number of our employees helped with installing the furniture, television sets, and bedding. One amusing facet from this experience was that several of us learned, for the first time, how to make a bed properly, with all sides even and every corner tucked.

As more than 500 people came to celebrate the 24th anniversary of Dudley Products, Inc., we also highlighted the occasion with a ribbon-cutting ceremony for Dudley's DCU Inn. The press proclaimed the fact that DCU was the only live-in residence of its type for cosmetologists in the United States. Its 45,000 square feet included a wing that served as dormitory space for up to 60 year-round students. The other wing was full-service, available both to the public and to the 100-plus students who come to the Kernersville campus for seminars. There was also space for a few corporate offices.

During the ribbon-cutting ceremony for the DCU Inn, several commentators talked about how Dudley Products sets an example for all of America. I couldn't have been more delighted. People had taken notice of our efforts to help others achieve economic empowerment and self-sufficiency. Ernie Sewell, then president of Branch Banking and Trust, which financed the deal, praised Dudley Products for persevering regardless of what the economic climate dictated.

"I look around me today, and I wonder where that recession is," declared Mr. Sewell. "I think we all see what can happen when a dream is backed up with lots of hard work. In fact, our bank had no qualms about financing this project, because we know the Dudley's work ethic."

In my follow-up to Mr. Sewell's touching appraisal of our company, I responded to his comments about our company's ability to grow in the midst of a recession.

"The answer," I said, "is that we simply don't believe in recessions. Instead, we choose to put our belief in God. After all, only God can make opportunities." I informed them that if we had worked according to the political, financial, or social climate of a man-made fate, then Dudley Products would probably have gone out of business years ago. "However," I said, "our chief business adviser and major stockholder is God. And, with power like that in charge, all we have to do is keep working, keep giving, and keep helping people. He has promised to take care of the rest."

Affirmative Opportunity

Tony Brown, the nationally known talk-show host and syndicated writer, was the keynote speaker at a banquet held later that day. Mr. Brown said that Dudley Products offered something to the black community called "affirmative opportunity." He explained that our company enabled people to get ahead while it put something back into the black community. Mr. Brown pointed out that blacks cannot prosper by continuing to leave 30 percent of their population in poverty.

I believe that affirmative opportunity evolves from a person's natural thought process. It cannot be achieved without there first being a commitment to self-reliance. You have to be committed to helping yourself before you can help others. Mr. Brown emphasized the importance of self-reliance among African Americans.

"Gone are the days of blaming others for our plight," he said.

I agree that as a race of people we cannot continue to be obsessed with racism. We must elevate our minds to a higher level, a level that surpasses inequality and injustice. Racism and bigotry will exist forever in the minds of some people, but we must recognize that racism is an illness—a sick way of viewing things. We cannot afford to be hindered by other people's illnesses any more than we can expect sick people to help us. We *must* help ourselves. That's self-sufficiency.

Dudley Travel Agency

After the opening of the DCU Inn, we took on another project. With enrollment at DCU growing close to capacity, our recruiters were spending an increasing amount of time making travel arrangements for our students. Our recruiters were working with local travel agencies, but coordinating the logistics of each student's arrival, stay, and departure from our campus was a time-consuming task.

We approached a local travel agency about the possibility of a business partnership. We believed that this arrangement would eliminate some of the difficulties our recruiters faced as they juggled their regular work with travel plans. In addition, we sought to earn a commission on the increasing amount of business travel we were pulling in. Unfortunately, our efforts to form a partnership with an existing agency didn't pan out. We certainly had enough travel volume between ourselves, our employees, and the students to justify having an in-house agency.

After weighing the pros and cons of such a move, the formation of Dudley's Q+ Travel Agency was under way. We hired experienced, eager travel professionals to manage the agency and handle the travel itineraries of all our employees, including the 150-plus national sales managers who were coming to Kernersville each month for sales meetings. The travel agency picked up some local clients as well. Although we hadn't anticipated expanding our company in this direction, we were pleased with the results. The travel agency is both detail-oriented and user-friendly. The "Q+" in it signifies the commitment to quality service espoused by every agent employed here.

The Yeates Center: "A Monument to Mother"

Our sales force rapidly increased to include more than 150 national, professional-only sales managers. Grateful and inspired, I continued to stage motivational sales meetings. At these meetings, everyone agreed that our company had a lot to be grateful for. Our salespeople were all doing well, and our corporate office staff continued to increase, while most companies had begun a shift toward re-engineering and downsizing. We had plenty to sing about. Accordingly, preceding each of our meetings, our fight songs resounded throughout our meeting rooms and into other parts of the building.

Unfortunately, the cold, unknowing environment of area hotels wasn't the appropriate place for the group songs and activities that had become a part of who we are. We needed a space that wouldn't constrain our excitement. All wanted to share their own personal stories and spread their excitement, but we needed an accommodating space in which to do it. If our meetings took more time that we originally planned, we needed a facility that would bend the rules and allow us to take as much time as we needed.

We needed a kitchen crew that would understand if our meetings ran ahead of or behind schedule. Instead, we were spending quite a bit of money holding our meetings in local hotels that didn't really satisfy our needs. Finally, we sought out a more cost-effective conference center. Initially, my wife and I were hesitant. Although we had never fully investigated the potential for using the abandoned building literally right in our backyard, we still weren't prepared for a revisit to the slate of challenges that had occurred during construction of the hotel.

On the advice of many people with whom we shared the idea, we agreed to give the reconstruction a chance. Recognizing the need to move quickly because of the money it would save us, we met with a number of employees willing to go about the task of tearing down cobwebs and clearing out trash in the old gymnasium. Sure, we could have paid someone else to do it, but we wanted our employees to have a first-hand experience in the process. This would be a history-making moment. Each of them could someday drive past the completed facility and honestly say "I helped them build it."

From an old gym of cold, concrete walls, we created the Yeates Convention Center. It has 7,000 square feet of space that can be easily conformed for seminars, exhibitions, receptions, and banquets. In addition, we've been able to use the center for a number of technical and broadcast productions.

The Yeates Center is also available to the public for private rentals. We have employed a sales and catering division, which offers assistance with coordinating a variety of special events, including corporate meetings, wedding receptions, and family reunions. While I must credit my wife with conceiving its name, her idea actually honors my mother. The building bears the maiden name of my mother, Clara Yeates. We planned the dedication ceremony to coincide with her 86th birthday in 1994. I was more than delighted at the chance to

146

present the Yeates Center to someone who had always had an unwavering faith in my ability to succeed.

I would be terribly remiss if I did not acknowledge the commitment made by my older brother, Clifton, an evangelist, for his looking after our mother. Cliff has devoted a considerable amount of his time and efforts to looking after mother personally in her golden years. It was Cliff who put aside his national commitments to come back to Aurora to help mother care for our father during the final months of his fight with leukemia. All the Dudley siblings are extremely grateful for his dedication and commitment, and also for the big-brother role he assumed while we were children. Cliff kept us on the strait and narrow path of what is right. We are all most grateful.

Breaking New Ground for the Glory of God

I was overjoyed at the success of our building efforts. With renewed vigor, we set out on our next goal. We planned to build a new corporate office and manufacturing facility on our land in Kernersville. We were cramped for space at the McCloud Road plant, and it was imposing serious constraints on the volume of products we could produce and ship each day. I feared that we might be unable to keep up with the demand. My wife worked with a team of architects to develop and complete plans for a new building. We were more certain this time about exactly what we wanted, and putting those desires in writing saved us a lot of time and energy.

In late September 1994, amid thunderous applause, my wife and I dedicated our new 80,000-square-foot headquarters to the glory of God. I assured our employees that the $3 million facility represented an important step in the strategic repositioning of our company. It would allow us to operate more cost-effectively. We could run a more efficient operation and produce a higher volume of products on a daily basis. The expansion would also enable us to hire a number of new employees.

At the opening ceremony, Eunice won over support from the

crowd by adding that "What makes Dudley Products so successful is not the bottles or jars that contain our products. It's not even the products themselves, because many of our competitors have similar things. It's our spirit that makes us number 1. We know how to take what we've got and make what we want out of it."

She was right. Only because of our spirit of achievement and faith in God had we landed in this new community, humorously referred to as "Dudleyville." I say humorously because Kernersville, N.C., is now our hometown. The great people of this community welcomed us with open arms.

Kernersville Responds

All of the growth we experienced during these years was just incredible. Rarely were we given enough time to think through all that was happening before the doors were opened to us. We acted on every opportunity that presented itself. We moved on faith each time there was a new challenge put before us. There comes a time in everyone's life when the blessings just seem to fall like rain. I am convinced that you have to be ready to act on them. There's often no time to analyze and plan. You have to *ACT* while the getting is good. As the adage says, "When the praises go up, the blessings come down." By the grace of God, every endeavor we approached seemed to be a gold mine waiting to bring forth profits. We had a wonderful new facility, larger staff, and incredible financial growth.

We were on our way to making the small town of Kernersville the "Cosmetology Capital of the World." The townspeople seemed to share our excitement about this prospect. Eunice and I were honored as their first "Citizens of the Year" in 1993. Being the third-largest employer in Kernersville, we assumed an active role in the town's Chamber of Commerce and its plans for economic development. But getting an award was the farthest thing from our minds. It was a pleasant surprise.

I remember the day Eunice mentioned having received a phone

call asking her to make sure that I was at the awards banquet. Since neither of us had any idea it was for Citizen of the Year, Eunice hadn't made the caller any promises. She knew that I kept a fairly busy schedule and couldn't be present for every program we were invited to attend. Instead of confirming, Eunice just said that she would do her best to get me there. As it turned out, my schedule was free on the day of the program, and we decided to go. I was astonished to learn that I was the recipient of the award. It was a real tribute to receive the award from my business and personal neighbors in our small town. I was gratified by their show of support. This proves that faith not only can move mountains; it can also build buildings and relationships.

Irene Parson

Cosmetology Instructor
Dudley Cosmetology University
Kernersville, N.C.

I am old enough to know and understand how God works. He works in mysterious ways. And at times we do not understand.

He loves to work through people whom he touches and he chooses. God chose Mr. and Mrs. Dudley to do his mighty works.

God's amazing grace touched the Dudleys to give practically my entire family a job. He touched the Dudleys to trust and take a chance on our son, who many believed was mentally retarded and would never get off Social Security.

Well let me tell you: While nobody else would take a second look at our son, let alone give him a job, it was the Dudleys who reached out and said "We'll work with him; we'll give him a chance." And I can witness today that our son is one of the best plant employees the company has, all because Mr. and Mrs. Dudley are all about helping people.

Wait until I witness this to you: I owe my very life to Mr. and Mrs. Dudley. I was running a successful salon in Indianapolis, Indiana, in the early '80s, and heard about Dudley Products through Roy Williams. On my own, I would arrange to go to whatever trade shows the company was doing and show up in its area. I enjoyed the energy that came from the people so much that I would help to do whatever needed to be done, without being asked. Each time I went back home, I felt better for having been with the Dudleys.

Let Faith Move Your Mountain

Mr. Dudley noticed me and asked what I did for a living. We talked briefly. He was interested in my story, and wanted me to visit the home office, which had been relocated to Greensboro. I told him that I would be happy to make the move there if he wanted. Mr. Dudley then had my husband, Ralph, come to North Carolina for a month, to see whether he was also interested in Dudley Products. He helped out in the accounting area, that being his background, and consented to both of us moving to North Carolina. We moved to Greensboro. A short time later, I was diagnosed as having cancer. We did not have the proper health insurance, and were faced with some tough decisions. We just didn't know what to do, so we went to Mr. and Mrs. Dudley for advice.

They told me to do what God would have me to do and not to worry about a thing. They said that the faith that I had shown in the company in helping at shows and coming to North Carolina more than earned the loyalty that they could show now in the time of need. They told me to go to the hospital, have the necessary surgery, and no matter how long it took, they would pay me and I would always have a job awaiting me when I came back. I came through the surgery successfully, and was determined not to stay away from work for six months.

The mental strength I received from knowing that Mr. and Mrs. Dudley were in my corner buoyed me through the recovery process. I was looking forward, moment by moment, to my return to work. I had to come back, in any way possible. I might not do the normal things I had done, but I had to return to work. So Mr. and Mrs. Dudley allowed me to go into the plant, sit down at the filling line, and cap bottles. This kept my spirit alive; kept me feeling that I was contributing; kept me looking forward to the next day. Through the encouragement that Mr. and Mrs. Dudley gave me and my family, I was off from work for only six days.

Had it not been for Mr. Dudley's touching me with human compassion and his desire to save a life, and Mrs. Dudley's driving in a snowstorm to come to the hospital to sit with me, and tell me not to give up, I would be dead today. I realize that when I remember the woman who shared the hospital room with me. Her ailment was less serious than mine, but she did not get the positive encouragement from a strong support structure as I did. She died within a few days of entering the hospital.

That was in the early '80s, and my health today is very strong. My doctor's quarterly report shows that the cancer is gone. I am healed completely; there is no trace of cancer.

To Mr. and Mrs. Dudley I say: You helped save my Life. Thank you. Thank you. Thank you!

11

Make a Difference in the World

In 1994, North Carolina Governor Jim Hunt commissioned a small group of people to serve as his advisors on the potential for building a business relationship with Africa. I was asked to join that group and participate in a tour of that continent to build economic ties between North Carolina and its developing countries.

During my time in Africa, I was able to visit a few hair-care professionals. I learned the plight of their businesses and the challenges they faced. As I listened to their stories, I contemplated ways that my company could help cosmetologists in Africa.

I also met President Robert Gabriel Mugabe of Zimbabwe. Mr. Mugabe is the first black president of his country, the former British colony of Southern Rhodesia. He and I shared similar beliefs about economic empowerment for black people. President Mugabe wanted to learn more about my company and discuss ways that we could do business in Zimbabwe.

I hadn't considered expanding our business to an international level so soon. We had discussed the idea, but only as a consideration for long-range planning. Then I learned that other hair-care companies in America were marketing their products in foreign countries. Their efforts to make products available were met with a lot of enthusiasm, for cosmetologists in foreign markets had been dealing with a shortage of good products for a while. When products were introduced into Africa, for example, the cosmetologists relied on their availability as a means for developing and improving business in their salons.

However, many were faced with the same challenge their peers in the United States faced. These companies had come in promising professional-only products, but after a short time they began to retail their products to a variety of stores. The public was pitted against the cosmetologists, for most people saw no need for professional care.

The other difficulty was that the cosmetologists were not receiving decent training on the use of the products. I sympathized with their plight, and after more careful consideration, I concluded that Dudley Products had to do something.

We formed the Dudley Products International Exchange and Development Program. Its goal was to seek out companies and individuals who wanted to help the people of Africa and other regions. Participants in this program joined me on a fact-finding mission to Zimbabwe. Once there, we each shared our technical and professional expertise with the residents of that country. With our group assembled, I reminded them that "We each have something unique to offer: the teaching of skills that will empower whoever has the desire to succeed." And, that would be the basis for our visit.

I also stressed to everyone that this mission was about much more than hair care. Dudley Products would bring to the table educational opportunities in hair care, salon management, and related areas. Other program participants were expected to offer knowledge and resources in their fields as well. The people of Zimbabwe needed motivation and business skills.

"Our aim should be to give something back to the Motherland," I said. "It's unfortunate that while our African brothers and sisters are struggling because of a high unemployment rate, we at Dudley Products are claiming to be job makers and not job takers. We have an obligation to share our knowledge and help them."

Dudley Beauty Schools in Zimbabwe

On our visit to Zimbabwe, we were met with overwhelming enthusiasm. One of my goals on this trip was to meet again with President Mugabe. I had developed an idea on how Dudley Products might play a role in the economic development of Zimbabwe. I proposed to His Excellency a joint venture between our company and the Harare Polytech and Chinoyi Technical Teachers College in Zimbabwe. More specifically, I suggested that we be allowed to start a department of cosmetology within the college to educate residents on hair care and business ownership. Dudley Products would teach hair-care skills and provide hands-on training to students interested in owning salons. The success of our graduates would create opportunities for them to train and employ others.

Everyone was excited by my proposal, so before boarding the plane back to America, I extended an open invitation to President Mugabe to visit Dudley Products. He would have an opportunity to see our corporate structure and manufacturing facility, and to speak with the students and faculty at Dudley Cosmetology University. If he was impressed by our operation, then we could further explore this development initiative.

President Robert Mugabe Comes to Kernersville

A few months later, President Mugabe and a 40-member entourage from Zimbabwe arrived in North Carolina. Included in his group were about 20 cosmetologists and business owners from Zimbabwe. I shared with them our commitment to build a solid partnership with cosmetologists. I also talked about things we could do together in Zimbabwe. I assured them that we would never go back on our promise of offering an exclusive line of professional-only products. Subsequently, Mr. Mugabe and I, along with a team of advisers, business executives, and professors from the Harare College and DCU, laid out plans for the new department of cosmetology.

Having the President of Zimbabwe in Kernersville was an historic occasion, and to underscore the importance of his visit, we coordinated several events to foster business networking opportunities with civic and community leaders who were unable to participate in our International Exchange and Development Program. We also were hosts to a business luncheon with state and local business leaders.

At this luncheon, President Mugabe offered a list of ways the attendees could expand their businesses into his country. In addition, we brainstormed and suggested a variety of economic development initiatives that Zimbabwe could employ, based upon our strategies here in America. During a black-tie banquet in our Yeates Convention Center, President Mugabe was our featured guest speaker. He entered the building surrounded by secret-service agents and a host of delegates from Zimbabwe. During his speech, the president talked about the prospects for future development involving our company. Not only were a host of state and local political figures in attendance, but also present was the late Dr. Betty Shabazz, wife of Malcolm X, the slain civil rights leader.

In his closing remarks, Mr. Mugabe told our guests that visiting Dudley Products was special because it illustrated the efforts of several people coming together with the common vision of creating "opportunities for black people to get ahead."

He told us: "The secret to lasting and meaningful economic development lies in teaching young people the important virtue of self-reliance so ably demonstrated by Joe Dudley." To say the least, I felt extremely grateful. The opportunity to branch into Zimbabwe was just another extension of Mr. Fuller's dream of raising people.

Brazil—and We Are Learning to Speak Portuguese

Shortly after the visit of President Mugabe, one of our employees, Neville Evans, suggested to me that we also consider branching out into Brazil. Neville had some professional contacts in that country who could help us get started. Realizing that DCU had graduated several classes of Brazilian cosmetology students, I was open to the idea of helping the people there.

In October 1995, a group of people from the Dudley Products International Exchange and Development Program ventured into the country on yet another fact-finding mission. Our host was Mr. Jimi Lee, a friend and business associate of Mr. Evans. Upon our arrival, Mr. Lee was quick to emphasize his frustration with the way cosmetologists in Brazil were being treated by other hair-care companies. Specifically, very few American products were being imported into the country, and the availability of those products was very inconsistent. Not only were the cosmetologists finding it increasingly difficult to stock complete product lines, but also, none of the companies that made their products available provided any education on their proper use. Mr. Lee and I agreed that under these circumstances, cosmetologists were not being empowered.

"Unlike those companies," I told Mr. Lee, "Dudley Products has always been dedicated to the education as well as technological advancement of cosmetologists. We could offer the cosmetologists top-quality, professional-only products and see to it that their supply was plentiful. In addition, we could provide them with an education in hair care and proper use of chemical products, business skills, and principles that ensure their success as salon owners."

During our visit in Brazil, we learned that cosmetologists in that country were not required to be licensed. There were no industry-wide standards for them to comply with. But it's easy to distinguish the cosmetologists with education and product knowledge from those who don't have it. It is obvious in the styles they create, the products they use, and the condition of their client's hair.

Dudley's Global Mission

Our primary mission in the international arena is not just to sell our products. The products are simply the means to a more important end. Our goal is to empower people and aid in their education and opportunities for economic development. We are building leaders. We are sharing a vision and developing a philosophy of commitment and a culture of self-sufficiency. We are teaching respect, giving encouragement, and showing support. We first develop the people internationally, bringing their educational level closer to the norm for the United States and Europe. This will help us sell our products successfully to customers who know how to use them, thus allowing us to have repeat and satisfactory sales.

Brazilian Cosmetologists Come to DCU

To this end, I invited five of the best cosmetologists from Brazil to enroll in Advanced Training Classes at DCU. This is an entry-level training program for licensed cosmetologists with previous salon experience. It includes a full curriculum that covers theory, product knowledge, and an exclusive hands-on training approach for all relevant styling techniques. Upon graduation, all the Brazilian students were challenged to share what they learned with other hair-care professionals in Brazil. I asked them to encourage other cosmetologists to come to DCU for advanced training.

Bridging the International Gap With Love

In the meantime, I sent a team of employees, faculty, and comsmetology graduates from DCU to Brazil. They were charged with responsibility for recruiting eager cosmetologists to enhance their skills by attending cosmetology workshops and classes through the Senac Technical School. The actual response was overwhelming, and to us it illustrated the Brazilian's deep desire for education. We made a commitment to help them as much as we could.

In addition to training the cosmetologists, we also set up a sales-management program to ensure adequate and timely distribution of our products to the salon owners who had completed their educations.

Other graduates from our program were hired as instructors for our workshops and classes at Senac. Undoubtedly, everybody is pleased with results of our International Exchange and Development Program. Dudley Products has expanded our dedication to education and business development to include a host of foreign markets, including Zimbabwe, Brazil, Martinique, Guadeloupe, Jamaica, Canada, and the Bahamas. Yet, this is only the beginning for us.

Bridging the International Gap With Relationships

I mentioned earlier the importance of developing associations and relationships with individuals or organizations that share your goals or objectives. Our international missions are no exception. I have been blessed to meet and become friends with a number of people around the world, especially in Brazil and Africa. A perfect example is my friendship with Mr. Ismail Kalla in South Africa. Mr. Kalla had nine brothers and sisters, and all were very active in his family-owned haircare business. The business has between 400 and 500 employees and an annual revenue of $100 million. I have been a guest in his home on many occasions, and he has suggested a number of ways that Dudley Products Company can make a difference in his country. Through positive relationships with other concerned people, we increase our knowledge and our ability to help others. This is true nationally and globally.

Looking Within Made a Big Difference in Me

Terrie Clawson
Vice President of Educational Services
and Director of Dudley South America

I'm living a life that most would not believe possible. Living and learning about life with a guardian angel to direct my path. That guardian angel is Mr. Joe L. Dudley, Sr. Let's see if I can help to paint a picture of my guardian angel.

I was blessed to be born to a mother, Mrs. Betty Clawson, who had a vision for her children. A mother who worked day and night to provide a positive, nurturing environment for my sister Sherri and me. When I was ten, she saw the need for a change in her life, and through an act of God and my uncle was introduced to Mr. Dudley and the Dudley Products family. She was given the opportunity to be a door-to-door branch manager in Charlotte, North Carolina. This position gave her the freedom she needed and an opportunity to bring us into a business setting.

From that point on, my world and the world of most of the children in the company became an ever-changing array of knowledge, excitement, and opportunity. Mr. Dudley always believed that if children had a good understanding of what the parents were working to accomplish, family harmony would be stronger. Sometimes children help parents stay focused on their goals.

I was encouraged to learn bookkeeping at the age of ten. This gave me a greater appreciation for money and the understanding

160

that it had to be managed. By age 12, I was an independent financial consultant for some of the salespeople. I would receive their weekly earnings, pay their outstanding bills, make deposits to their savings accounts, and give them allowances. For some it was difficult to accept this from a 12-year-old, but after they saw the results, my age became unimportant.

When I reached high school, I officially became a Dudley employee. I worked as a store clerk, receptionist, bookkeeper, and payroll clerk. During this time, I was also involved in many school and after-school activities, including the following:

- *Girl Scouts*
- *YWCA Youth Club*
- *Three years of Junior Achievement, in which I was, in successive years, secretary, then president, then vice president of the company we formed*
- *German Club*
- *Cheerleader*
- *Choir*
- *Distributive Education Clubs of America (D.E.C.A.)*

During this time, Mr. Dudley would plant seeds of a bright future in all our minds. He had contests and prizes for grades and school attendance, and for those of us who would sell door to door. He even had a junior sales force that took trips to different cities and amusement parks. He encouraged the older children to lead these programs and be examples for the younger children. This mentoring and grooming helped me to realize that, through persistence, hard work, and faith, all things are possible and obtainable.

I moved to Chicago at age 17, after completing high school. I sold products in our Direct Sales Division. My friends often asked whether I had any fear or reservations about being away from home and being in the big city. I loved living in Chicago. I firmly believe that home is wherever I make it. Mr. Dudley taught us that people are people wherever you go, and there is nothing to fear but fear itself.

Being flexible and open-minded to change can take you a long way. About two months after I started in direct sales, one of the individuals that worked in the home office left. Because of my previous experience working with my mother in Charlotte, the company felt that I was a good candidate for the open position. I was moved into the office as a secretary.

One day Mr. Dudley asked me, "What are you doing with your life?"

In the past, because of work and school, I had little time for devilment. But when I moved to Chicago, my day would end at 5:30."

"Terrie," Mr. Dudley said, "you know an idle mind is the devil's workshop." So he sent me to school. I worked during the day and went to school at night.

Over the succeeding few years, I have had numerous wonderful and challenging opportunities, including working as an accountant, trade-show manager, office manager, sales representative, travel coordinator, hotel manager, director of advanced training for DCU, and vice president for educational services. With every new opportunity, Mr. Dudley would send me out on faith. He believed that I had within me what it would take to succeed, even when my belief in myself was weak and faltering.

Out of all of the positions and opportunities I've had, I feel that the most rewarding and life-changing is my current position. It has been a Godsend, but at first I did not know it. When in the presence of wisdom, most often we don't take full advantage. In my case, it was a lack of understanding.

*Some years ago, Mr. Dudley had Lester Brown give seminars to the sales force. Mr. Brown spoke of three things that helped to explain my last two years: **conditioning, comfort zone,** and **removing the blinders.***

*He said that we have been conditioned to think and act in certain ways because of our environment. I understood and agreed, and also felt that my **conditioning** had been of a positive nature. So I felt that in this area I was OK. The second was **comfort zone.** That's when he began to step on my toes. Because of the success and op-*

*portunities I had at an early age, I felt very comfortable with who I thought I was. The third was **removing the blinders**. Many opportunities are missed because of our focus, because of our conditioning, because of our fear of stepping out of our comfort zone.*

In 1994, Mr. Dudley was introduced to Jimi Lee, who had many years of experience working in the cosmetics industry in Brazil. He told Mr. Dudley of the problems the Brazilian cosmetologists were experiencing and how education by Dudley Cosmetology University could change their lives. Mr. Dudley went to visit Brazil, where he met some of the top cosmetologists in the country. He invited them to come to Kernersville to have the DCU experience and to brainstorm on the needs of the industry. From this came the International Exchange and Development Program.

At the university, we had many international groups attend, but for some reason I was attracted to this group. Portuguese is their native language, but communication was not a problem. I felt compelled to be with them morning, noon, and night.

One day, Mr. Dudley asked if I would like to work with the Brazilian market. My first thought was that I was being sent away, but my answer was yes. At that time, I needed a challenge and a change. I was operating only in my world, my comfort zone, my cocoon, not the real world. Again he sent me on faith, keeping the promise he made to God early in his life. His promise was: "God, if you help me get out of the situation I'm in, I'll spend my life helping others."

I found myself in a new country and new culture, using a different language, and totally different business practices. But I tried to operate as if I were in my old environment and nothing had changed. Consequently, I produced no results. There was conflict in my environment, and all that I had learned over the years had been tucked away and neatly stored. In the Bible it says "In all thy getting, get understanding." I could not understand why they just didn't understand me.

I came to the realization that nothing would change until I changed myself. I picked up a book Mr. Dudley had given me, titled

The Seven Spiritual Laws of Success, *by Deepak Chopra. I had read this book more than two years previously, but did not get the true meaning. This time, I started reading and came across a passage that said: "The relationship that I have with others is a direct reflection of the relationship that I have with myself." The blinder started to rise, and things instilled many years ago began to breathe life again. I read a little further, and it pointed out that "every seed is the promise of thousands of forests. But the seed must not be hoarded; it must give its intelligence to the fertile ground to unfold." I discovered that my giving had not been done freely; that it had been given conditionally. I was not giving, but investing, and expecting a return.*

Mr. Dudley had told me many times when I had conflict in my environment that with time I would understand. I would ask: "Why can't you just tell me?" He would say: "I could give you a response, but it would not be the answer because of acceptance." Thank you for being my guardian angel and pushing me to look within.

Search within yourself;
Draw your guidance from within;
Don't live your life in fear of sin,
Wondering if there's a Heaven or Hell to lose or to win.
Peace can only be found in harmony.
Be patient and humble;
Be gentle and meek;
Search inside yourself for all that you seek.
You can reach the ocean by many streams;
After that, all becomes one, it seems.

—Jimilii

Be a Bridge Builder

The Dudley Products Collegiate Sales Manager Trainee Program arose out of a series of discussions I held with two employees, Willie Bailey and John Raye. Each morning, the three of us would meet and enjoy a brisk walk. We had a rule some mornings that we would only discuss ideas with a value of a million dollars or more. One morning, our focus was on how we could recruit more young people into the company.

Dr. Bailey, a former dean of business education at a local university, said it shouldn't be a difficult undertaking. John Raye and I both looked curiously over at him. We knew Dr. Bailey to be a laid-back sort of person, but he'd made this statement with about as much ease as a person telling a joke.

"Listen, guys," he began. "Surveys say that there's a decrease in African-American students going to college and a decrease in the number graduating. Not only that, but other surveys say that when these students graduate from college, they have no job prospects."

He continued, "We already know that the number-one motivation for young people straight out of college is money, and we know that if they are not immediately locked into satisfying jobs, their learning stops immediately. So all we have to do is formulate a program that fills the voids."

As I began to process what he was saying, one question kept creeping back up.

"Dr. Bailey," I said, "you're the only one of us with a Ph.D., so can you explain what is going on to reverse such a negative situation?"

"There are a lot of very real challenges," he replied, "but few very real solutions."

Collegiate Recruitment and Training Program Started

Over the next week or so, we brainstormed this topic further during our morning walks. The result was our training program, designed to develop a strong economic base of young, talented entrepreneurs for the world.

For the first six to eight weeks of their employment, we work with the college students to enhance their leadership skills. We work with them on self-improvement and personal development. It is mandatory that they participate in the morning reading group. We challenge them to think independently and to take initiative. We also spend weeks canvassing neighborhoods, doing door-to-door sales. I lecture the students on the fundamentals of business and entrepreneurship.

The first group in this program comprised 27 students. They exceeded our expectations by completing their training ahead of schedule. A majority were hired as sales managers in our company. In keeping with my personal commitment to raise 200 millionaires, the collegiate program prepares young people for the opportunity and creates strong leaders.

Leadership Enhanced Through Direct Selling

I am convinced that the traits necessary for effective leadership can be enhanced through direct selling. It takes initiative and courage to approach complete strangers and open the lines of communication. It takes loyalty to the product or service you are trying to persuade others to use. Serving clients requires integrity. They have to trust you and depend on you to supply them with merchandise. It also takes insight. Many times in direct selling, you will have to know what products to recommend or the extent of the services your customers need. You may have to read their minds sometimes, because they won't always tell you what they need. In fact, they may not even know themselves until you suggest something. With wisdom from God, you can satisfy existing customers and invent creative avenues for getting new customers.

The development of strong leadership qualities is essential to the development of young entrepreneurs.

Willie Bailey, Ph.D

Special Assistant
to Joe L. Dudley, Sr.
Executive Director of Collegiate Program

I worked in the Winston-Salem community, which is less than ten minutes from Kernersville, for a number of years. Still, I didn't know very much about Dudley Products Company. I had served on local Boards with Mrs. Dudley, but I didn't know much about her or the company, except from comments I gathered here and there.

My first real contact with the company came several years after I accepted my position as head of the business division of a local university. Frustrated with the bureaucracy of the education system, I had come there with the desire to teach students and watch them grow professionally because of the knowledge I had helped them acquire. Also, like a lot of educators, I was constantly smacked in the face by a community of businesses that refused to employ the bright young minds I'd helped make ready for the world. What made it all the more disturbing was the fact that, as a teacher and confidant, it was difficult to detach myself from the students after they had completed our courses. I felt a personal disappointment every time one of them didn't go on to achieve the dreams and goals they had set for themselves.

Finally, I came to the conclusion that I had saved enough money to sustain my family for at least two or three years. I resigned from the university, opting to devote my time to finding the right niche for both my skills and my desires. No more "Jobs" for me, I'd decided.

Be a Bridge Builder

One evening, Dr. Horton, a friend of mine from the university, invited me to go with him to a session held every Tuesday night called "Mastermind—An Alliance." It was held at Dudley Products and was facilitated by a gentleman named John Raye.

Although I found the first session quite interesting, having a background in administration, I was slightly annoyed by the lack of organization. The meeting needed more structure, in my opinion, so the following Tuesday night I returned with two students, who kept minutes and assisted with recording notes on the flip chart. I became a regular at the Tuesday night meetings and, in due time, found myself actually helping John Raye to run them.

I eventually met Mr. Dudley. My initial impression of him was that he was different from most people. I knew that he was quite a busy man, and I was taken aback when he sat down to talk with me for nearly a half-hour. During that time, I shared a lot with him, from my obtaining a Ph.D. at age 24, to my tenure at the university, to my decision to leave and seek out a better opportunity for myself.

Mr. Dudley invited me to walk with him and John Raye some mornings, if I was available. He expressed an interest in hearing more about my desire to help students. I agreed to join them as soon as I had the time.

My first walk with the two of them was so invigorating that I almost begged to join them again sometime. Before I had the opportunity to grovel, an invitation was extended. I agreed to walk with them every day until my dream was fully developed and I knew what I wanted to do.

In the interim, I felt as though I was with long-time friends. Our minds had a certain synergy that enabled our ideas to mesh well. Perhaps, it was because we shared a lot of the same experiences from childhood. We were all reared in rural environments and seemed to face one handicap or another. I began to hang around the corporate office on a regular basis.

In addition to our morning walks, the 6:30 a.m. readings, and the Tuesday-night meetings, I would also come to the office on occasion just to see whether I could help out. Finally, Mr. Dudley men-

*tioned the words I wasn't ready to hear. He said, "Dr. Bailey, since
you're here so much anyway, I ought to just hire you and pay you a
salary."*

*"Oh my," I thought. "I've sent the wrong impression." Then I
told him, "I'm not looking for a job."*

*"Well, at least you let me pay you enough to meet your monthly
bills and cover your insurance costs," he offered.*

*Let me tell you that my greatest handicap has always been fail-
ure to recognize the opportunities right under my nose. Although I
had earned a Ph.D. at age 24, I never really set out to do that. Although I started out as an assistant professor, I quickly gained
tenure and ended up as the dean of the department in a university; I
never really set out to do that either. For me, it has always seemed
as though God didn't have time to wait for me to come around. The
opportunity was there, so he always just pushed me right into it.
And, I always surrendered.*

*Dudley Products was different. I wasn't so eager to join the
company, even though Mr. Dudley had laid the opportunity out before me. I was more than a little hesitant about doing door-to-door
sales, and I knew it was something he really believed in. I began to
think, "If Mr. Dudley isn't embarrassed by knocking on doors, then
why should I be?" So I set out to Charlotte, North Carolina to give
it a try. In time I developed the courage to go door to door even
where people knew me. I headed straight for the university.*

*By the end of the day I'd spent there, one of my former students
approached me, almost in tears.*

*"Dr. Bailey," she said, "I almost had a fight today because some
of the students were laughing at you." I calmed her down and assured her that everything was going well for me. I invited her to
come and visit me sometime—at Dudley Products, Inc. in Kernersville. Since that time, we have hired several students from the university, and that makes me feel good.*

*That experience helped me to realize that sacrificing my pride
was the small price I had to pay to recognize that I had found the
opportunity I left the university in search of. I am helping to create*

jobs for young people. And I'm doing it by example.

I, along with Mr. Dudley and John Raye, developed the Dudley Products Collegiate Sales Manager Training Program. I believe that God has been preparing me for this opportunity all along. I have the professional happiness I longed for in my life. I feel ten years younger, and I'm convinced that I have the power of God on my side. Thank you, Mr. and Mrs. Dudley.

A Look Toward the Future

A Morning Meditation (Excerpt)

Every morning is a fresh beginning.
Every day is the world made new.
Today is a new day. Today is my world made new.
I have lived all my life up to this moment, to come to this day.
This moment—this day—is as good as any moment in all eternity.
I shall make of this day—each moment of this day—a Heaven on Earth.
This day is my day of opportunity.

Hail to this Day
I look to this day for it is life—the very life of life.
In its course lie all the realities of existence.
The bliss of growth—the glory of action—the splender of beauty.
Yesterday is now a dream, and tomorrow is a vision.
Today well-lived makes of every yesterday
a dream of happiness and of each tomorrow a vision of hope.

This day is life's magnificent gift to me.

—*Author Unknown*

I think every day about where our company is headed. I know that every day is a chance to make a new beginning, a fresh start. The dawn of each day brings with it a wealth of opportunity. At Dudley Products, we are always ready to seize that opportunity. Our motto in

173

1995 was "Soaring to New Heights," and in 1996, "Goals and Profits Will Ensure our Vision for Tomorrow."

A lot of work is yet to be done. There still are people all over the country and the world who need encouragement. I strive to continue pursuing my objective of raising people, and I have more than 400 employees devoted to the same goal.

Committed to Continuing Ownership of Dudley Products, Inc.

Over the years, my wife and I have received many offers from individuals and investors seeking to buy our company. But we refuse to sell it. It's impossible to put a price on what we have at Dudley Products. We've been offered a large sum, but that doesn't even scratch the surface of what our company is worth. We have a commitment to our employees and to cosmetologists everywhere. We know full well that if we sold our company, in no time at all our products would be in retail stores all over the world, thus violating our partnership with cosmetologists.

In addition, our most loyal and devoted employees would be sent right out the front door in the name of re-engineering. There's no way Eunice and I could stand by and watch that happen. We are 110% devoted to Dudley Products, its employees and their futures. We are devoted to people in the world we haven't even met yet.

We are on a mission that will take us all over the world providing education and opportunity. As we strive to make our mark, we will continue to live and walk by faith that we can achieve every goal we set out to accomplish. Concerning Dudley Products, Inc. being for sale, I say, "You cannot put a price on a mission!"

Expansion of Partnership With Professional Cosmetologists

I have challenged the company to broaden our partnership with professional cosmetologists all over the world by giving them greater access to the Dudley Cosmetology Education System. Our goal is to provide the opportunity for interested individuals to become cosmetologists, and provide the opportunity for licensed cosmetologists to improve and enhance their skills. Education is critical to the continuing success of cosmetologists. We will help them learn the latest advances and trends in hair care and beauty aids, and also how to develop and enhance their business and management skills. We want everyone to be job makers, not job takers.

Other key partnership-development programs include our Dudley National Technicians and Ambassador program. Dudley Ambassadors, all DCU alumni, are nominated as such by their Dudley sales representatives. Our National Technicians are selected from our list of Ambassadors. Dudley Products very carefully chooses qualified cosmetologists to perform for the company in the prestigious position of DCU instructors and National Technicians. Dudley also provides an extensive training program for each Ambassador and Technician.

These are progressive cosmetologists who are committed to serve as positive role models in their communities and to promote the development of individuals, groups, and organizations in the art and science of cosmetology.

We have identified well over 300 Ambassadors, and our plan is to recruit many more to keep cosmetology a growing and profitable industry.

Cosmetics and New Training Focus

We also hope to open Dudley Beauty Schools all over the country. We believe that hair and skin care for men is just as important as makeup and beauty schools are for women. Barbers everywhere need to know that our partnership with them is on the horizon.

Dudley Products has unveiled Dudley Cosmetics, a fabulous new makeup line. This exclusive line features blush, eye shadow, cream foundation, liquid makeup, lipstick, translucent powder, pressed powder, concealer moisture stick, and other facial and nail products, all designed with women of color in mind.

The makeup business started out as a personal project, but we quickly realized that we had the talent and expertise in our company to take this initiative and run with it. We are doing makeup seminars all over the country, retailing our makeup line in our beauty schools and through the salons on our professional sales routes.

Our daughter Ursula doubles as our corporate counsel and director of Dudley Cosmetics. She recently married, and is quick to point out that while Mrs. Dudley is her mother, she is now Mrs. Ursula Dudley Oglesby.

We will also continue to market our new perfume line, which includes not only the perfume, but also cologne and dusting powder. This line of exciting products is named after our youngest daughter, Genea, who recently graduated from the Wharton School of Business in Pennsylvania. Genea works as a marketing executive in the company, and in 1997 entered the MBA program at Duke University.

Continued Support and Commitment Through "Dudley Moments"

Over the next few years, we plan to devote significant dollars to continuing our advertising windows called *The Dudley Moment,* on segments of the Black Entertainment Network's hit gospel telecast, The Bobby Jones Show. Through our "Dudley Moments," millions of people have learned more about our mission at Dudley Products. We have received tons of correspondence from people who have been inspired to achieve their dreams as a result of our series.

The five-minute windows give viewers a behind-the-scenes look at life at Dudley Products and has afforded us the opportunity to showcase the talents of some of the best cosmetologists around the world. Through the Bobby Jones Show, we are keeping the field of cosmetology alive.

Continue the Dream

Finally, my most personal desire and chief commitment is to carry out Mr. Fuller's dream to create 200 millionaires. We've already experienced a lot of success toward that goal. From the first day that we began our route sales program, we encouraged all sales managers to regard their territories as their business enterprises. We currently have more than 150 employees investing in the company's 401-K Program. Through continuous participation, and a good rate of return, they are on the way to achieving millionaire status and helping keep Mr. Fuller's dream alive. ***How to Become a Millionaire With 100 Customers*** is a tape I have done to help more cosmetologists become millionaires. It is also my hope that this book will be used as a training tool for future millionaires.

I am convinced that we will accomplish every one of these goals, and I'll tell you why I'm so sure of it:

We live and walk by faith, and we know that, through faith, all things are possible!

Lastly, I say, "In our time, and in our space, and with the grace of God, you and I can make a difference . . . if we continue to Walk By Faith!"

Final Thoughts

All meetings at Dudley Products end with these words, so too shall I end our meeting here.

> "When we can see beneath the evil
> All the golden grains of good,
> We will love each other better
> When we are better understood!"
>
> —*Sanskrit*

177

For Further Information

For additional information on Dudley Products, Inc., Dudley's products or cosmetics, Dudley Cosmetology University, Dudley College System or any services mentioned,

Please call
1-800-334-4150
or visit our web site
http://www.dudleyq.com

Recommended Reading List

If you want positive thinking to become a part of who you are, then agree to become an avid reader of good literature. Allow yourself to feel the words. It will help you to envision your goal. As ideas come to you, stop reading and write them down. Also, try reading aloud sections of those books that you find most appealing. There is greater impact in hearing yourself say the words. And, most important, apply what you read to your life. Always consider how the advice of the author can better serve you!

As a Man Thinketh, James Allen
How I Raised Myself From Failure to Success in Selling, Frank
    Bettger
Live Your Dreams, Les Brown
The Secret of the Ages, Robert Collier
Riches Within Your Reach, Robert Collier
Acres of Diamonds, Russell Conwell
The 7 Habits of Highly Effective People, Stephen R. Covey
Principle-Centered Leadership, Stephen R. Covey
Ten Days to a Great New Life, William E. Edwards
Think and Grow Rich, Napoleon Hill

Success Through a Positive Mental Attitude, W. Clement Stone &
 Napoleon Hill
The Law of Success, Napoleon Hill
Mastering the Art of Selling, Tom Hopkins
Succeeding Against the Odds, John H. Johnson
Think and Grow Rich: A Black Choice, Dennis Kimbro
The Greatest Salesman In the World, Og Mandino
The Power of Positive Thinking, Dr. Norman Vincent Peale
Enthusiasm Makes the Difference, Dr. Norman Vincent Peale
How To Be a Great Communicator, Nido Qubein
Professional Selling Techniques, Nido Qubein
Stairway to Success, Nido Qubein
Tough Times Never Last, But Tough People Do, Dr. Robert H.
 Schuller
Move Ahead With Possibility Thinking, Dr. Robert H. Schuller
Think Like a Winner, Dr. Walter Doyle Staples
The Success System that Never Fails, W. Clement Stone
Dave's Way: A New Approach to Old Fashioned Success, R. David
 Thomas
22 Immutable Laws of Marketing, Al Reis & Jack Trout